ESG

# THE GORBACHEV CHALLENGE AND EUROPEAN SECURITY

A Report from the European Strategy Group

Nomos Verlagsgesellschaft
Baden-Baden

CIP-Titelaufnahme der Deutschen Bibliothek

The **Gorbachev Challenge and European Security:** A Report from the European Strategy Group / ESG. – 1. Aufl. – Baden-Baden: Nomos Verl.-Ges., 1988
ISBN 3-7890-1655-1
NE: European Strategy Group

1. Auflage 1988

Contents Page

*Preface*

I.

This *Report* is published under the auspices of the European Strategy Group (ESG). Hannes Adomeit (Stiftung Wissenschaft und Politik, Ebenhausen) acted as general editor.

II.

The European Strategy Group was founded in 1985. It is funded from private sources. It was established to facilitate, coordinate and generate security studies in Western Europe, in particular on a multi-national scale. It brings together senior experts from a variety of disciplines and national research institutions specializing in foreign and defence policy studies. Currently, it draws its membership from France, Britain, Italy, the Netherlands, Norway and West Germany. At this stage, research institutes represented in the ESG are the Royal Institute of International Affairs (RIIA), London; the Institut Français des Relations Internationales (ifri), Paris; the Istituto Affari Internazionali (IAI), Rome; the Norsk Utenrikspolitik Institutt (NUPI), Oslo; and the research institutes of the Deutsche Gesellschaft für Auswärtige Politik (DGAP), Bonn, and the Stiftung Wissenschaft und Politik (SWP), Ebenhausen.

The chairmanship of the ESG, as well as the responsibility for programme management, is rotating on a three-year basis. At present, the SWP in Ebenhausen is providing this function with Uwe Nerlich as chairman. Additional standing members are Pierre Hassner, Karl Kaiser, Laurence Martin, Sir Ronald Mason, Thierry de Montbrial, John Roper and Stefano Silvestri. Holger Mey is serving as executive assistant.

The purpose of the ESG is threefold, namely

- to provide a framework for collaborative European reseach on European security, Atlantic affairs, and East-West relations;
- to direct its work both towards the study of broader strategic concepts and the assessment of policy issues, as well as to initiate and coordinate major European research efforts, which no individual institute would usually be able to undertake;
- to engage in a series of joint projects with the Aspen Strategy Group (ASG) and within the European-American Institute for Security Research (EAI).

The ESG is thus committed to two kinds of major activities:

- European projects
- joint European-American projects.

For the European projects, task forces with leading European experts are assembled for a given subject, with one or two of the institutes involved providing the project management. The task force report is periodically reviewed by the ESG and ordinarily supplemented by an ESG policy paper.

III.

The Report consists of the ESGs Executive Summary and Policy Recommendations (Part One) and the Analysis (Part Two).

In the prepartion of this Report, in particular the Analysis, the ESG drew on a task force, consisting exclusively of West European Sovietologists and analysts of East-West relations in Europe. It included Hannes Adomeit, who acted as chairman of the committee; Jane Hamilton-Eddy (Soviet analyst, London); Philip Hanson (Centre for Russian and Eastern European Studies, University of Birmingham); Pierre Hassner (Fondation Nationale des Sciences Politiques, Paris); Vladimir Kusin (Radio Free Europe Research and Analysis, Munich); Malcolm Mackintosh (former advisor on Soviet affairs to the International Institute for Strategic Studies and the Cabinet Office, London); Michel Tatu (*Le Monde*, Paris); Nils Morton Udgaard (*Aftenposten*, Oslo); and Franz Walter (specialist in Soviet defence economics and military strategy at Industrieanlagen-Betriebsgesellschaft, IABG, Munich).

Additional contributions to the task force's work were made by Pierre Lellouche (ifri), Friedemann Müller (SWP) and Peter Volten (University of Utrecht). Alex Pravda (RIIA) provided useful comments to the drafts of the Report.

Input papers were extensively discussed by the task force at meetings at ifri in Paris, in June 1987, and at RIIA in London, in September 1987, and in several ES executive sessions. The final version of the Report was reviewed and approved by the ESG in April 1988.

IV.

The ESG gratefully acknowledges the substantial organisational and editorial service provided by Hannes Adomeit, as well as his and the task force's patient and painstaking analytical work. It also expresses its great appreciation of the support granted by the Ford Foundation.

Ebenhausen, May 1988

# Part One:

# Executive Summary and Policy Recommendations

## *I. Assessing Change in the Soviet Union*

Any discussion about Western security should address (itself to) the questions: What are the threats to our security? Against whom and what are we defending ourselves? Soviet military power and the Warsaw Pact continue to be regarded in the West as the main threats to Western security so that developments in the Soviet Union, as well as in Eastern Europe, must be carefully studied.

Without change in the Soviet system Soviet propensities toward military self-restraint are unlikely to grow. However, change may deemphasize the role of military power. Moreover, it may also help to render the Soviet Union more competitive. Military self-restraint *prior* to systemic change, which will obviously take a long time, would be an encouraging sign of policy change, but is unlikely to occur. The issue, then, is whether the political and economic context of Soviet military power has begun to change in ways that might eventually induce military self-restraint and whether there are chances for the West to reinforce such developments. This implies that Western security policies should be pursued within a policy framework facilitating responsiveness. The construction of such a framework evidently requires both analysis and good judgment.

The Soviet Union has not made it easy for the West to reach balanced judgements. The extreme secrecy, the continuing repression of its citizens, the military show of force in Eastern Europe and Afghanistan, and the frequently hostile attitude displayed toward the West -- all these factors tended to reinforce negative views about the country, its system and its policies.

But Soviet policies are not immutable and cannot be divorced from developments within the Soviet system or elsewhere in the world. The system is rigid, but it is not simple; problems are chronic in nature, but they have differed over time.

Thus, prior to Gorbachev's ascendancy to power several major attempts had been made to adjust the Soviet system to new domestic and international realities. Such attempts included the New Economic Policy (NEP) after 1921; Malenkov's "new course" after Stalin's death in 1953; and Khrushchev's combination of de-Stalinisation and Soviet-American detente in the late 1950s and early 1960s. In all of these cases, efforts at reform were made both in domestic and foreign policy. The Brezhnev period produced another variety of adaptation: foreign policy detente without domestic reform.

But none of these changes led to a fundamental and lasting connection of the Soviet Union with the established international political and economic order. Rather than contributing actively to maintaining the status quo, Soviet foreign policy remained committed to its destruction and the establishment of "universal communism".

It is not surprising, then, that in the West policies towards Moscow during previous Soviet reform efforts were at the centre of policy making. At the same time their formulation was subject to controversy. As for the current efforts, how should one interpret the developments? For some observers a number of new approaches and trends in Soviet domestic and foreign affairs do exist which, if they were to continue, would amount to a major change in the character of Soviet policy. Other analysts, although discerning new approaches, doubt whether a "reformist" leadership will be able to overcome the inertia of the system and the opposition of various groupings and state bodies.

## *II. The Soviet System and Soviet Politics before Gorbachev: Constant Features*

Although the basic structural elements of the Soviet system are well known it is useful briefly to enumerate some of them. This may be of particular benefit to those Western political leaders and commentators who are inclined to see the Soviet Union as a country just like any other. Certainly the room for manoeuvre for the Soviet leadership in security policies depends on the objective constraints and pressures inherent in the Soviet system and the subjective dimension. Any major departure from a tested and proven course will be difficult and meet great resistance.

We are confronted, firstly, with a basic ideological tenet, namely that a state of "irreconcilable contradiction" exists between East and West. This is subscribed to by the CPSU as a whole, not only on theoretical grounds but also for the very practical reason that the party bases its claim to exclusive political power on the differences between the two political systems. Ideology and power are intertwined. If either one is affected or weakened, far-reaching reforms and decay are likely to transform the political system, or a "strong leadership" will be called for to restore the status quo.

For these reasons past foreign policy *vis-à-vis* the West had little flexibility. In the Soviet Union, normalisation of relations and mutual cooperation were held to be only of a "temporary" and "tactical" nature. The dangers of ideological "contamination" and of the loss of power for the CPSU were seen as constant threats.

This essential limitation to engaging the West in the politics of détente has been accompanied by a second major and constant feature of Soviet politics: the longing for recognition as a true superpower. One can scarcely underestimate the collective oversensitivity of the Soviet leadership to any indication that the Soviet Union and the "socialist community" were not in fact the equals of the United States and its Western European and Japanese allies. But statements, such as the one made by Gromyko in 1968, that "no matter of importance can be decided without, or against the will of, the Soviet Union", reflected more the desire for power and influence than reality. This was due in part to the Soviet neglect of instruments of influence and control other than military power. Increasingly it became obvious that the Soviet Union was not able successfully to compete with the West ideologically, economically, culturally, and politically. Unrelenting (military) efforts of the Soviet Union to compensate for these deficiencies may have been understandable, but they clearly were at odds with a policy of détente.

This leads to a third point on which there was a consensus in the Soviet Union: the utility and purposes of military power. Unlike in Western liberal and democratic society, military power has been regarded by successive Soviet leaderships not as a "necessary evil" or "blemish" but as a useful and morally ("historically") justified instrument. They have considered the armed forces as providing Moscow with increased power and influence in world affairs, guaranteeing that gains can be made and consolidated in the Third World, affecting the domestic politics and foreign policy orientation of Western European states and inducing the United States to recognise the Soviet Union as an equal. Consequently the West has been warned repeatedly that the existing balance of power will never be allowed to change to the detriment of the Soviet Union, regardless of the extent of Western defence efforts or the economic sacrifices the Soviet Union had to make. The high degree of consensus between the party and the military on this subject has enabled successive heads of the general staff to argue for nothing less than a war economy. And when it came to the defence effort attempts at moderation could be expected to be opposed by a powerful coalition of the military and orthodox party apparatchiki.

A fourth, closely related and continuous feature in Soviet foreign policy of the past decades has been the prominent position which the United States has played in Soviet perspectives. Western Europe is probably still the most important *prize* of Soviet diplomacy. But it is the ordering of relations with the United States by means of which Soviet leaders have endeavoured to change their influence in Western Europe as well. For example, Brezhnev's visit, in October 1981, to Bonn -- prior to the beginning of negotiations on intermediate range nuclear forces in Geneva -- was first placed in the context of Soviet-American relations and was only subsequently evaluated for its contribution to relations between the Soviet Union and West Germany. Recent statements do nothing to indicate a diminished interest in the United States as a superpower. On the contrary they are a reaction to what the Soviet leaders have perceived as an intransigent stance adopted by

Washington; they are responses also to currents in Western European countries which seek to moderate such a stance.

A final constant feature of Soviet foreign policy has been the objective of preventing war. There is no reason to assume that Soviet leaders have not been aware of the risks of a war with the West, and of the danger of annihilation if war were to break out. Hence there has been a recurrent readiness to engage in arms control talks can be partially explained by their wish to prevent dangerous developments from arising in the arms competiton. This does not, however, elevate arms control to the level of a goal per se. Arms control, for the Soviet Union, has always had a political purpose. Thus, for instance, the SALT I agreement meant, among other things, the visible inclusion of the Soviet Union in the ranks of those countries with which the United States was prepared to entertain equal, business-like relations. In later phases of Soviet policy, notably in the context of the controversies surrounding the enhanced raditation weapon and the stationing of intermediate-range nuclear missiles in Europe it had meant, or had seemed to signify, a larger degree of influence in Western European security affairs.

Seen against this background of constant features, what are the main changes that have occurred under Gorbachev? And what is their rationale?

## *III. Summary of the Analysis*

### 1. Economics

#### a. Rationales and Directions of Change

The primary impetus and main justification of change in the Soviet Union undoubtedly lie in what Gorbachev has called "precrisis" conditions. By this he appears to have in mind not only ideological ossification, social decay and international isolation but most of all serious stagnation in Soviet economic development and, consequently, the inadequate performance of the Soviet Union in the East-West economic and technological competition.

The important questions to be asked in this context consequently are as follows: What measures does Gorbachev intend to take in order to achieve a "radical turn" in economic affairs? What are the relations he envisages between economic reform and changes in society, domestic politics and foreign policy? Finally, what are his chances of success?

The Soviet leadership will probably achieve some improvement in economic affairs over perhaps a five-year period. This view is based on the premise that changes in priorities and personnel can have more than a short term (up to two years) effect.

Gorbachev, to provide some detail, is presiding over a switch of resources into research and development plus production engineering; these are the sectors which generate most new technology associated with manufacturing processes. For the time being, prioritity is apparently to be given to the production of investment goods in order to modernize the equipment within the machine-tool sector itself. One cannot expect the pay-off to those additional resources to be as high as it would be under competitive capitalism, but it should at least be positive. If the resource shift occurred mainly at the expense of projects of the kind exemplified by the BAM railway and the Siberian river-diversion scheme, it could even be fairly painless.

Similarly, increased pressure and personnel changes may well be capable of generating more output from given inputs, without changes in the system, simply by reducing organizational "slack". The amount of slack relative to potential output by the end of the Brezhnev era was by general consent large, and there is no strong reason to assume that its reduction is a process that would take place within a short time scale.

Only recently has Gorbachev presided over measures of economic re-organization that could be called radical. In late June 1987, a package of semi-market reform measures was adopted by the Party's Central Committee, after considerable and difficult debate. The measures taken consisted in a new law on the state enterprise and a statement of intent about further, complementary changes in the organization and functions of central administrative bodies in the economy. In combination with earlier measures, intended to encourage family enterprises and small cooperatives, this batch of laws and decrees aims at a curious kind of half-way-house economic system. What is envisaged is *not* a market-socialist reform such as the Hungarians aimed at in 1968 (and which have not been fully implemented twenty years later). It is, nonetheless, a radical departure from Soviet practice of the last fifty to sixty years.

The Soviet reform process might over time become more radical. It might even prove possible to invigorate Soviet performance in innovation while retaining predominantly socialist ownership and the party's monopoly of political power. But "reforms" are unlikely to have much impact on performance in the foreseeable future (up to the end of 1990), except insofar as the encouragement of small-scale private and cooperative ventures outside the planning system produces some improvement in everyday life for Soviet citizens -- a development which would be of no direct and very little indirect consequence for Soviet foreign policy. The other changes are not meant to be operational before 1991.

An objective test of the success of Gorbachev's economic strategy will be the Soviet share of Western imports of manufactured goods, which at present is small and has, in fact, declined since the mid-1960s. Joint ventures with both East European and Western concerns can now be formed in the Soviet Union, the Western joint ventures being subject to mandatory Soviet majority shares. "Western" joint venture legislation already exists in all the East European countries except the GDR, and in several cases has been in place for over a decade -- yet without producing dramatic results. The Soviet objectives in these organizational changes seem to be chiefly to promote non-fuel exports for hard currency, and to get better access to Western technology and mangagement skills. But the exercise rather resembles the science-and-technology agreements with Western firms, which were supposed to have a great influence on East-West trade and Soviet economic performance in the 1970s but which, in fact, had very limited success.

The present Soviet strategy relies more heavily than before on cooperation within the Council of Mutual Economic Cooperation (CMEA), and keeps "dependence" on Western technology at a modest level. In the mid-1980s Soviet planners seem to have regarded machinery imports from the West as equivalent to about one-tenth of their annual investment in new machinery, and imports from Eastern Europe as equivalent of about one-fifth. The volume of machinery imports from Eastern Europe had been rising faster than that from the West during 1981-85, and it appears to be Soviet policy to continue along those lines. However, the East European capacity to deliver a sharply increased volume in 1986-90 is much reduced because of the very low level of investment in Eastern Europe since the late 1970s (and that quite apart from the quality issue). Furthermore, Soviet ruble earnings in Eastern Europe will be reduced by the delayed effect of the 1985-86 fall in oil prices, since energy looms large in Soviet exports to CMEA as well as to Western countries. The reduction of the big accumulated East European debt to the USSR in the next few years (from which Poland is spared until 1989) goes some way to offset this effect, but in general the Soviet ruble capacity to import from Eastern Europe will not be strong. The pressures leading the USSR back to more intensive development of trade with the West are obvious, but so are the impediments.

Another test of success in Gorbachev's economic strategy would be the degree of satisfaction on the part of Soviet military planners with the military technology available to them in the mid-1990s. That test, however, will be even more difficult for outside observers to apply.

A strengthening of the Soviet "challenge" in the longer run is more likely to be achieved by a strategy which includes a short-term, relative decline in the priority given to the military: not necessarily an absolute cut in the military effort, but a period in which the resource allocations to the military are somewhat less than they would have been on previous policies. There is no way of being certain that Gorbachev and his associates share this view, but there are some signs that they do.

b. Defence Spending

As for trends in military spending, Western estimates are that the average annual growth rate has become markedly lower since the mid-1970s (2 percent in constant prices) as compared to the preceding decade (4-5 percent). Measured in current prices, the share of defence expenditure in the Soviet GNP (by Western definition) has continued to increase, from an already high number of 12-14 percent in the early 1970s to about 15-17 percent at present. This is almost three times the corresponding share in the United States. Both the size of, and the increase in, the Soviet defence burden seem to suggest that the long-term policy to let military outlays grow faster than GNP cannot be sustained.

It is too early to assess a "trend" of defence spending after Gorbachev's access to power. There has been some dispute among Western experts as to whether and how much Soviet military expenditures have increased in 1983 and 1984, and whether one could speak of a new upward trend after 1982. The dispute has made it clear that intelligence estimates have to be judged with caution and used with care. On the basis of the most recent figures, and despite some reservations about their validity, it appears that since 1985 no significant change has occurred in Soviet military expenditure.

Possible effects of growth or cuts in military spending can be analysed with the aid of econometric models. Such models reveal a curious asymmetry: when defence spending grows by a constant rate, economic growth will develop in an exponential fashion as more and more resources are withdrawn annually from investment funds. When, on the other hand, defence spending is reduced by a constant rate, economic growth will develop only in a logarithmic fashion as relatively fewer resources are added to investment funds. On that basis one may conclude that there is only a limited incentive for the Soviet government to reduce defence spending so as to enhance economic growth; there are comparatively stronger reasons for avoiding larger allocations of resources for military purposes.

Economic performance, as both the model and common sense suggest, can only be improved by far-reaching economic and political reforms. But in that case it would be difficult to estimate the effects of deep cuts in military expenditure: the present "war economy" could then be lessened, leaving more room for satisfying the needs of the consumer. Such a development would transcend the parameters of the model which aims at approximating the functioning of the current system.

Furthermore, it is by no means certain or even probable that the Soviet leadership regards cuts in military spending as a tool for enhancing overall economic performance. By cutting defence spending it may have in mind more specific yet nevertheless important effects such as improvements in certain key sectors of the economy. As mentioned, modernization of the economy, but particularly of the machine-tool sector, is a major objective of the Gorbachev leadership. Hence, if scarce high-quality materials and high technology components (e.g electronics) were used to a lesser extent for the production of weaponry and made available for the production of investment goods, modernization of important economic sectors could conceivably be promoted.

The defence industry, which has for a long time been engaged in the production of a whole range of civilian goods, might have to expand this very role. In fact, such an expansion appears to be the easiest and most effective method to achieve a certain transfer of productive capacity from the military to the civilian sector.

Insofar as cuts in defence expenditures are concerned, several distinctions need to be made. It is necessary to separate short-, medium- and long-term effects of reductions, as well as to distinguish between the effects of cuts in nuclear and conventional forces. Savings could result from the stretching of procurement, and research and development programmes; manpower reductions; and curtailment of operations, maintenance, exercises and training.

As for procurement costs, cuts in *nuclear* forces are unlikely to produce direct financial benefit let alone significant reductions in the level of defence spending. Decommissioning costs for strategic systems are heavy and would offset the financial gains of operating and maintaining a smaller force. Verification, when it includes on-site inspection, could also prove expensive. But even in the long term the savings would be modest. This is due to the relatively small share of nuclear forces in overall military expenditure and to the requirement of modernization of the remaining force.

More substantial savings could be made in the *conventional* field. This is because of the concentration of expenditure (approximately 80 percent) on general purpose forces. Furthermore, considerable scope exists for savings given the significant Warsaw Pact superiority over NATO in weapons stocks of many types and the long-standing Soviet inclination to pursue simultaneously, on a belt and braces principle, more than one programme for a single, or for closely related, purposes.

But major savings will most likely materialize only in the long run. In the short run one might even expect overall military expenditure to rise in real terms by some 2.5 percent over 1987-1992, with growth of weapons procurement even increasing at a higher rate. This projection would be based on the fact that for most weapons systems the period from conception to obsolescence lasts many years; and that almost all major weapons, for which procurement and operational expenditure are likely to be incurred through the early 1990's, are already known.

This projection presupposes that established patterns are not altered by policy changes. But even with a change of course and the cancellation or reduction of weapons programmes in scope and time, costs in terms of wasted resources still tend to be considerable given that decisions have been taken to move from the research stage to development, and that heavy outlays have been incurred for buildings, manufacturing equipment and prototypes. For these reasons and because of the long lead times in fielding new equipment, cutbacks now would not yield substantial savings until the 1990's.

As for cuts in the size of the Soviet armed forces the cost/benefit analysis must be equally complex. On the one hand, the potential savings on personnel costs are relatively small given existing pay levels of a largely conscripted force. Personnel costs currently account for only about 8 percent of the total budget. Also there is considerable benefit to the economy from the training given to conscripts as, for instance, familiarity with certain technological and management skills which are of use when conscripts are released back into the labour force.

On the other hand release of manpower could aid economic development. Given labor shortages in industry any sizeable addition to the civilian labour force should be welcome to Soviet policy makers.

All remaining possibilities would yield only marginal savings. Most of the expenditure on operations and maintenance goes on spare parts and servicing, and cutbacks on a major scale would prove counterproductive.

Overall there are advantages and possibilities for cuts in the defence effort, and there are, therefore, incentives for arms control. In the short term the release of manpower can help alleviate problems caused by an acute labour shortage. Transfer of resources from the military to the civilian sector can serve to reduce important bottlenecks. In the long term the channeling of scarce resources and personnel to strategic sectors can aid the process of modernization and even improve economic growth. Most important, arms control can assist in preventing an acceleration of the military-technological competition with the West and an even sharper reversal in Soviet economic fortunes.

These considerations raise questions as to the scope for change in the Soviet Union under Gorbachev, given the existing domestic political conditions.

## 2. Domestic Politics

### a. New Developments

It is, of course, not the first time that a leader in Moscow has tried to improve and modernize the Soviet system. Parallels and similarities with Khrushchev's reformist efforts in the 1950s and the 1960s are evident. But there are also important differences. First, the context has changed. When Stalin died in 1953, the Soviet economy had not exhausted its capacity to ensure "extensive" growth by the extraction of more raw materials and the migration of more peasants to the cities. Today the Soviet leaders are confronted with a scarcity of raw materials and labour resources, and they have to acknowledge the fact that economic stagnation has brought about a general deterioration of social conditions.

A second feature distinguishing Gorbachev's approach from previous attempts is the realisation that economic progress cannot be made by mere bureaucratic reorganization of the management system but that it needs to be supplemented by invigoration ("democratization") of Soviet politics and society. In that respect "de-Stalinization", which has come again to be the order of the day, may outwardly be less dramatic than its counterpart under Khrushchev but it is also broader and deeper.

A third new feature is the emphasis put by Gorbachev, especially after the June Plenum in 1987, on the private sector, its potential role in agriculture as well as in the development of services and light industry. Here Gorbachev goes further than any of his predecessors since the promulgation of the New Economic Policy (NEP) by Lenin in 1921. But this emphasis has to be translated into realities, which is still far from evident at this point.

A fourth important achievement distinguishing Gorbachev from previous leaderships has been the extensive reshuffle and renewal of cadres at all levels. This was expected after two decades of stagnation and "petrification" under Brezhnev. But its breadth and the rapidity with which it was implemented were both unexpected.

A fifth new factor is the fact that the influence, impact, and visibility of academic specialists with training in complex analysis has increased. There has been a shift away from ideologists towards problem-solvers.

Sixth, the new party leader has extended the scope of human rights in the Soviet Union. He has allowed Andrei Sakharov to leave exile, granted pardon to well-known dissidents, and allowed many of them to emigrate and some of them to return. Under his tenure the number of exit visas granted to Jewish "refuseniks" and new applicants has increased, and so has the rate of emigration of ethnic Germans.

The seventh and most striking aspect of Gorbachevism is *glasnost* or the policy of "openness". In practice this means the opening of new areas of information and comment. It also means more scope to address social issues, an extension of the targets open to criticism, including the military, and, at least in one case, the KGB. More significantly, it has opened the way to a new appraisal of history with a renewed wave of de-Stalinization, a veiled criticism of collectivization, a new more positive judgement on Khrushchev and radical criticism of stagnation under Brezhnev.

b. Limits of Change

But these assessments pointing to major change have to be qualified. Many basic features of the Soviet system remain, and so do the obstacles to comprehensive reform. Thus the Central Committee is still not the decision making body which Gorbachev probably would like it to be. It remains the most important concentration of the high-ranking *nomenklatura*, a place where dissent can be aired and objections raised. But more than half of the full members have carried over from the Brezhnev period and of the 1981 Party Congress, more than a third were there ten years ago, and one tenth are septuagenarians of the "Stalin generation". This explains why Gorbachev has demanded that a party conference be convened in June 1988. But a struggle has started already to decide whether that conference will be entitled to elect a new Central Committee, as the General Secretary wants, or to make only minor changes in this body.

The composition of the Central Committee, in terms of its functions and the distribution of its membership between party and government officials, the military, and representatives from other institutions, is almost the same as it was in 1981. Turnover of personnel has been more rapid than before, but constituencies and their respective weight have remained basically unchanged. The stagnation rate, i.e. the percentage of leaders having the same position today as at the end of Brezhnev's rule five years ago, is higher in the provinces than in the center. The main exception to the rule is Central Asia where majaor replacements have occurred. By contrast, the leaderhips in the Ukraine, the Baltic states and Azerbaidzhan have been remarkably stable.

The Politburo remains the main political decision making body, as well as the only place of true debate. Its composition has significantly changed. But this does not mean that all new members of the leadership are Gorbachev's supporters on each and every issue. The Politburo most likely contains a combination of various groups, or loose groupings, representing different emphases of political commitment.

Basically everybody in the Politburo seems to agree that Brezhnevite stagnation cannot be allowed to continue and that there is no alternative to change. There is certainly an overwhelming majority in favor of discipline and the corresponding campaigns already begun under Andropov. A majority probably also supports economic reform despite the many differences as to modality. Thus *perestroika* has become a generally accepted frame of reference. But some political leaders have a very narrow conception of change. Others support the principle of *perestroika* but are against it in practice. The latter, i.e. those who are advocating a slower pace of change (the "socialist conservatives"), apparently asserted themselves successfully in the second half of 1987 but have lost ground in the Spring of 1988.

While change in one form or another is supported at the top of the party leadership, and is very much endorsed by the large majority of the cultural and technical *intelligentsiya*, this is less true for the middle and lower levels of the party. At these levels conservatism and braking mechanisms are more pervasive, as may be found in the various layers of the economic bureaucracy. In order to overcome such difficulties Gorbachev would certainly like to mobilize working class support. But this would require measurable improvements which have not, as yet, been delivered.

There seems to be a change of attitude of the KGB towards Gorbachev and his policies. Initially, the KGB was clearly allied with Gorbachev for his having supported Andropov's policies. But with the touching of many taboos in Soviet ideology and the revelation of the ugly features of Stalinism, past and present, the KGB in the long run cannot hope to escape unharmed. This may explain the change in mood among the "Chekists".

The relationship between Gorbachev and the military too is sensitive and significant. When Gorbachev assumed power in March 1985 he inherited a rather tense relationship between the party leadership and the armed forces. Since then he has adopted some measures to lessen the internal conflict but has taken others which could reignite it. Certainly his vigorous stance for modernization of the Soviet economy must appear to them as welcome. They also realise that only a revitalised economy is able to sustain modern armed forces.

Since 1986, Gorbachev's demands for *perestroika* in the armed forces have become more insistent. After the CC plenary meeting in January 1987 and the "Rust affair" in May of the same year party control over the military has been more strongly reasserted. The military is no longer exempted from harsh criticism concerning internal discipline and morale, performance in training and exercises, and use of economic resources. In personnel policy the rate of turnover has accelerated. The previous, demonstratively privileged, position of the military in society and politics has been scaled down. Finally, Gorbachev has allowed and initiated a discussion of international security and military doctrinal affairs pointing in the direction of a complete revision of well established strategic thought and military postures.

Such trends, however useful for foreign policy and propaganda purposes some of which may be, are clearly of concern to the traditional military officers; their latent dissatisfaction and resistance is one of the factors which lessen the chances of a comprehensive reform process.

Nationalism in non-Russian areas is also a potential focus for opposition. Since Gorbachev's ascendancy to power there have been numerous manifestations of non-Russian and, at times, anti-Russian nationalism. Its disruptive potential is indicated by the fact that demonstrations, some of which unprecedentedly large, have taken place in Lithuania, Latvia and Estonia, as well as in Armenia and Azerbaidzhan. The Crimean Tartars and ethnic Germans have become more restive. In this context, the argument of the "conservatives" that *glasnost* is not a necessary corrective of, but a dangerous stimulus to, national unrest is also likely to have retarding effects on comprehensive reform.

The lifting of taboos has left untouched large areas of public life which are still covered by secrecy. *Glasnost* has not had a big effect in the provinces. No major changes have taken place in the management of the media and culture, nor in the way in which editors are appointed and decisions made. With the exception of some cracks in the wall of secrecy, mainly in the context of arms control, the most important aspects of military affairs remain concealed. This concerns the size and composition of the military budget, the strength, organization, and deployment of the Soviet armed forces, the priorities in military research and development, the scope and rates of weapons production, and the volume, composition and distribution of arms exports. The decision making process at large, including the discussions in the Politburo and other internal debates as, for instance, at the

Central Committe plenums, remain unpublished. In foreign policy new initiatives are still being announced after they have been decided.

## 3. Foreign Policy

### a. "New Thinking" and New Flexibililty

As with most other countries which have embarked on major domestic change, foreign policy in the Soviet Union under Gorbachev is an area where continuity is the rule rather than the exception. In fact, given the strategic and geopolitical position of the Soviet Union and its role as a superpower, the current Soviet leader will most likely pursue objectives and goals similar to those adhered to by his predecessors.

Yet it would have been surprising if the new dynamism and the demands for new solutions to old problems in the domestic sphere had not found their counterpart in foreign policy. And indeed they have.

Under the heading of "new political thinking" significant "creative adaptations" of ideology and concepts of international security are taking, or have taken, shape. Current trends are pointing away from orthodoxy, rigidity and antagonism to a more benign and cooperative inflection of "peaceful coexistence". Universal problems and interests are said to exist which require common solutions. Foremost among them is the avoidance of nuclear war. To that extent ideological reformulation is beginning to emphasise that peace has priority over the class struggle.

Related to that is the idea of interdependence. Security has been acknowledged by Gorbachev, at the 27th Party Congress and thereafter, to be indivisible. No country, he said, could hope to achieve it at the expense of the other; only mutual security could realistically be aimed for.

Yet another change in the ideological underpinning of Soviet foreign policy is the notion that security in the nuclear age "cannot be safeguarded by military-technical means alone"; that it "is also a political task"; and that this task could not be achieved from "positions of strength". Gorbachev has also authoritatively stated that in the nuclear age war is "inadmissible". Taken to its logical conclusion this would render obsolete all the previous elaborate Soviet distinctions between "just" and "unjust" wars.

Previously the concept of the "correlation of forces" was an important, or perhaps even the decisive, operational principle on which Soviet foreign policy was based. Today the discussion of its relevance is muted. But where such discussion does take place, the significance of military elements is being downgraded; conversely, the importance of economic factors is receiving greater emphasis.

Yet the process of ideological adaptation and change is still contradictory and incomplete. Some aspects of the "new thinking" are not at all new. Other aspects are not credible as a manifestation of genuine change. No explicit statement exists as to what was wrong with the "old thinking". There is still ambiguity as to the precise status of the world revolutionary goal of "universal communism". All the main "antagonisms" are still considered to be operative: social, intra-state, inter-state, transnational, those between the "three power centres of imperialism" (the United States, Western Europe and Japan), and between socialism and capitalism. Finally, "imperialism", according to the revised CPSU programme and the main documents of the 27th Party Congress continues to be regarded as inherently "aggressive" and to be the chief source of war. Only hesitatingly and infrequently a question mark is being raised as to whether this is still true.

Nevertheless, the processes of ideological adaptation and revision point in the right direction and are perhaps even now capable of making some impact on Soviet foreign policy practice.

Another change, and one that can be noted both conceptually and in practice, concerns the primacy of Soviet domestic over Soviet foreign policy. Gorbachev and his advisors are conscious of the fact that reform and modernization of the Soviet economy must primarily be an indigenous effort, and that overextension and overcommitment abroad can be costly and risky, and detract from this effort. Mainly as a result of successful domestic transformation do they hope to improve again the image and influence of the Soviet Union in world affairs.

But the relationship also applies in the opposite direction: success in the improvement of the Soviet Union's prestige abroad can help Gorbachev contain the criticism at home; the more progress he can make in Soviet-American political relations, arms control and crisis management, the more secure will be his own domestic position. Since in foreign policy decision making he does not have to contend with a similarly vast and powerful bureaucracy as in domestic politics, Gorbachev may increasingly look for possibilities to enhance his standing by activism abroad.

Even now it is quite apparent that, as in domestic politics, the skill and sophistication in foreign policy has improved. The advice Gorbachev receives is likely to be more professional, and less dogmatic and ideological than in the past; previous failures and present realities are more realistically taken into account. The new team of foreign policy makers seems to be more conscious of the erosion of the effectiveness of traditional instruments in Soviet policy toward the West. They apparently realize, more clearly than their predecessors, that the communist parties are of dubious value when it comes to influencing Western government policy. They are certainly conscious of the fact that the strength of the "peace movement" in Western Europe has waned. They are, therefore, more prepared to deal with such forces as are representative of the political mainstream in the West, above all and preferentially, the social democratic parties, the liberals -- and the conservatives.

The costs, benefits, and risks of expansionism in the Third World are also seen in a different light today than in the 1970s. In order to reduce the economic "costs of empire", contain the political repercussions of the use of force, notably on the relationship with the United States, and lessen the risk of counterintervention or counterrevolution supported by Washington, the Gorbachev leadership seems to consider it appropriate to avoid new commitments -- above all new *military* involvement. At the same time it is still clinging to most of the global positions gained by its predecessors, attempting to consolidate those gains and making them less risky and costly.

Avoidance of new commitments is evident in the Middle East, in Nicaragua and South Africa, where militarily Moscow has adopted a low profile. Safeguarding the positions reached had been charactersitic for the Soviet stance in Afghanistan, until about the autumn of 1986. Since then, not least as a result of American arms shipments, notably the Stinger anti-aircraft missile, Gorbachev has steered a steady course towards withdrawal; the April 1988 Geneva agreement suggests that he may even be prepared to accept a collapse of the Marxist-Leninist regime in that country.

Another indication of new approaches in foreign policy is Gorbachev's attempt to build up a wide network of diplomatic contacts and to enhance the Soviet diplomatic, political and cultural presence in countries and organizations in which it was hitherto underrepresented or not represented at all. An indication of this policy, at the international economic level, is the interest Moscow has expressed in joining, in one form or another, the General Agreement on Tariffs and Trade (GATT) and the International Monetary Fund (IMF), and the apparent readiness not only to come to legal agreements but also to a *political* arrangement with the European Community.

b. Regional Issues

At the regional level, Gorbachev has, in the wake of a programmatic statement on Moscow's Asian policy in Vladivostok (July 1986), endeavored to mend his relations with the Chinese leadership. He has moved in one way or another, even if perhaps only symbolically, on all the three points which, the Chinese have claimed, stand in the way of an improvement of Sino-Soviet relations: the Soviet occupation of Afghanistan; the presence of Soviet troops along the Chinese borders, notably in Mongolia; and Moscow's support for the Vietnamese occupation of Cambodia.

More flexible tactics can also be observed in the Middle East. Moscow has made concessions on the Egyptian debt, leased tankers to Kuwait, acted as mediator for the Palestinians, persuaded Syria to show more moderation, extended feelers to Israel, and consented to a significant increase in the rate of Jewish emigration. In the Iran-Iraq war, without abandoning its traditional support for Iraq, it has sought to improve its relations with Iran and cautiously avoided being drawn into the taking of sanctions.

The main feature of Gorbachev's foreign policy, however, has been the emphasis put on the reordering of relations with the United States. Initially, until the autumn of 1985, it had seemed that priority would be given to the European connection. Thus even before his formal inauguration as General Secretary, when he visited London in December 1984 at the head of a Soviet parliamentary delegation, he spoke of Europe as "our common house", implying that the United States, as a trans-Atlantic power, really had no business in that house.

However, a privileged relationship with Western Europe did not materialize. Thus far, some progress has been made concerning the establishment of legal and organizational ties between CMEA (Council for Mutual Economic Assistance) and the European Community but the conclusion of corresponding agreements has been held up by the Berlin problem. Nothing has come of Gorbachev's feelers concerning the establishment of relations with the Community at the political level. The "common house" has continued to be plagued with the traditional panoply of separate national interests and identities -- in the East as well as in the West.

In fact, the Eastern Europen countries now differ from each other and from the Soviet Union more than at any time in their common communist history. Hence, Gorbachev faces a cluster of different, nationally determined problems which produces different, nationally determined responses to his "new course".

Gorbachev seems aware of the fact that, apart from heightened national economic predicaments, systemic obstacles and the disunity of reformist purpose, there are also severe deficiencies in "socialist economic integration". There is ample reason for such awareness. Today, in Eastern Europe "direct links" and "joint enterprises" are largely felt to be centrally imposed undertakings that have little to do with the real needs of the participants, and which therefore bring few benefits. Today, there seems to be a recognition in Moscow and in Eastern Europe, that joint scientific and technical advancement, along the lines of the December 1985 CMEA plan, cannot be achieved.

As internal economic pressures continue to mount the Eastern European regimes are likely to seek ways to reduce the share of the "costs of empire" imposed by Moscow on its European glacis. This too puts them at odds with the current Soviet policy, which aims at importing qualitatively better industrial products to help in the development of the Soviet economy rather than seeing them exported to the West.

A withdrawal of a substantial number of Soviet troops and their equipment from Eastern Europe may well be on Gorbachev's agenda. But constructing a new cost-benefit analysis of the utility of military power in Europe will obviously not be an easy undertaking. Perceptions of Soviet withdrawal could lead to instabilities: Even if it may not look that way now in some countries, there is a higher potential for the advancement of reformism in Eastern Europe than in the USSR. And if, as a result, the sparks of reform were to ignite an explosive outburst in Eastern Europe, Gorbachev could see himself faced with the same problems of intervention, and threats of intervention, as his predecessors.

All of these difficulties in Soviet-Eastern European relations put limits on the scope of change in "Europe, our common house".

Consequently, the major results of the first three years of Gorbachev's rule cannot be found in Soviet-Western European relations but in the improvement of relations with the Reagan administration -- the Soviet-American summit meetings in Geneva, Reykjavik and Washington, the agreement on the elimination of intermediate-range nuclear missiles, and the plans for yet another summit (in Moscow) with the aim of reaching an agreement on the limitation of strategic weapons. The purposes of Gorbachev's appeals to Western Europe, therefore, have most likely not been aimed at separating the USA from Western Europe (this could only be a very long-term objective) but to influence, through the Western European connection, the direction of American policies towards the Soviet Union.

### c. Arms Control

Change can also be observed in Soviet arms control policy. At its root probably lies a reassessment of the utility of the arms competition, above all, in the nuclear sphere. Starting in the late 1970s defence outlays in the United States had begun to rise sharply. New challenges were issued to the Warsaw Pact in the form of more sophisticated conventional weapons and Reagan's Strategic Defense Initiative. In conjunction with the deployment of intermediate-range nuclear weapons and the resulting capability of NATO to strike at Soviet territory from Western Europe, as well as the on-going US strategic modernization programmes, it was the Soviet Union that was put into a position to react. Furthermore, Moscow felt constrained to respond in the field of high technology in which it could compete less easily and effectively. Gorbachev has begun to draw the appropriate conclusions from such actual and potential developments and to adjust his arms control agenda, so as to regain the initiative.

He has returned to the complete and comprehensive disarmament theme prevalent under Khrushchev. But in contrast to Khrushchev the new party leader has combined comprehensive disarmament propaganda with new approaches to specific arms control negotiations; their most important result so far is the December 1987 Washington agreement to remove an entire class of weapons.

Gorbachev has broken entirely new ground on the inspection issue. For decades the stubborn Soviet refusal to agree to reliable on-site control and verification procedures had been a major stumbling bloc in East-West arms control. Today the principle of inspection has been conceded. New precedents have been set. The first dim outlines of *glasnost* in other military affairs are now beginning to become visible. He has made some unilateral gestures of restraint -- some of dubious value.

The General Secretary has also initiated, or encouraged, a new discussion of military doctrine. This includes the idea, first raised in the West, of "reasonable" or "sensible" sufficiency of military forces, the aim of achieving security at lower levels of armament, and the removal of the imbalances in some categories of weapons not through an increase by the side that is behind but by reductions of the side that is ahead. The discussion includes assertions to the effect that, historically, strategic defence at times (e.g. in the 1943 battle of Kursk) proved superior and even decisive against offence, and that in contemporary conditions the "military-technical aspect of military doctrine" should have a primarily defensive direction. Similarly, the idea has been put forward to eliminate the possibility of surprise attack; to reforge and reposition forces so as to achieve a mutual "structural inability to attack" -- a term first coined by West German social democrats.

If such doctrinal revisions were to become generally accepted the road could be wide open for major changes in the Soviet force posture in Central Europe to be effected either unilaterally or through arms control. As if to begin the corresponding journey, at the Conference on Disarmament in Europe (CDE) mandate talks in Vienna on conventional stability, the Soviet Union has agreed to Western demands to consider the elimination of the capacity for surprise attack a major negotiating objective. However, in the military journals, articles on conventional *offence* still predominate and thus reflect continued Soviet force developments. Scepticism in the West concerning conventional arms control is warranted because of the past experience with the talks on mutual, balanced arms reductions (MBFR), where the Soviet Union has rejected the Western aim to eliminate invasion capabilities, and by recent comparisons of certain categories of NATO and Warsaw Pact weapons provided by the Soviet defence minister, General Yazov, in February 1988. Finally, doubts about the purposes to be pursued by the discussions on defensive conventional postures are fed also by frank admissions of Soviet spokesmen that the mere *proclamation* of a defensive doctrine is already having, from Soviet perspectives, salutary effects in international relations.

How, then, in the light of the developments in Soviet ideological, social, economic and military affairs, and in foreign policy, should the West react? To answer this question requires a fresh look at the changing *Western* context.

## *IV. The Changing Western Context*

During the 1970's, the era of détente led to much argument among Western political leaders and experts in the field of East-West relations as to Soviet goals. By and large Moscow was given the benefit of doubt; actual or incipient changes in the Soviet Union in directions favourable to the West were not ruled out. But in the second half of the decade hopes to that effect gave way to the realisation that Soviet policies had taken a turn for the worse. The Soviet leadership under Brezhnev appeared to be returning to militant, orthodox ideology and foreign policy expansionism. A more or less consistent development was seen ranging from the support of Cuban intervention in Angola and the Horn of Africa, to the support given to Hanoi to enable it to achieve victory in South Vietnam, to intervene in Laos and to occupy Cambodia, and culminating in the Soviet intervention in Afghanistan. Arms control, which had seemed so promising to many observers in the early 1970's, proved to be increasingly difficult, not in the least because of the apparently unrestrained military build-up in the Soviet Union. Rigid behaviour began once again to characterize Soviet foreign policy towards the West. On the domestic scene the leadership failed to adjust the Soviet economy and society to new challenges, increasingly letting the system slide into political immobilism, economic stagnation and social decay. The Soviet leadership it seemed had foresworn change.

During the short reign of Andropov Western observers were suddenly confronted with a number of changes. These concerned vigorous efforts aimed at improving economic performance by means of a campaign for more discipline, shifts in personnel at the higher levels of the party and state, and calls for more initiative and responsibility at lower levels of the party and state apparatus, as well as at the workplace. Soviet interpretation of events in Eastern Europe, notably in Poland in 1980-81, as well of the ills of the Soviet economy, became more realistic. Although Moscow adhered to its intransigent stance in foreign policy, Western observers began to believe that change, at least in Soviet domestic politics, was now more likely. After the brief return to the "stability of cadres" and other business as usual under Chernenko, Western reactions to the new style as well as new policies of Gorbachev have appreciably altered.

Today many Western analysts of Soviet affairs, and political leaders in their wake, no longer regard as inconceivable that a fundamental shift in Soviet domestic and foreign policy may be taking place; that "restructuring" in internal affairs and "new thinking" in international politics may combine to produce an entirely different Soviet Union than the one the West was confronting in the past. As in the past disappointment could, of course, succeed the present excitement. But if current trends are extrapolated they could lead to significant shifts in Western public opinion.

These trends in perceptions of the Soviet Union occur simultaneously as concern has been growing in Western governments and the defence community about an erosion of previously agreed security policy and military doctrine. Concerns about solidarity and the collective defence of the Western alliance have been expressed since its inception but several new developments have taken place which tend to complicate matters.

To be enumerated among them are trends of American unilateralism or, concerning the superpower relationship, bilateralism. As time passes, such trends however slow in themselves, may cause a change of a structural nature. Reykjavik is an example of this. Europeans are well advised to regard it not as an unfortunate incident but as an event consistent with a gradual but unmistakable shift in American strategic thinking.

The Washington summit meeting of December 1987 and the conclusion of the agreement on intermediate-range nuclear missiles are also events which one might perceive as a signal of new or revived bilateralism between the two superpowers. Stronger American emphasis on global responsibilities outside NATO and growing interests in the Far East also bear on the trans-Atlantic relationship. In the field of economics, too, American policy has shown a tendency towards unilateral decisions and actions in spite of recurring Western economic high level meetings. The huge budget and trade deficits of the United States are bound to affect Washington's foreign policy and are, in addition to the present economic consequences, likely to complicate intra-alliance political relations.

Diversity and divergence of national views on a range of issues, both intra- and extra-alliance, also make it difficult to formulate a coherent Western European security concept. This confusing state of affairs is aggravated further by a new phenomenon, namely the manifest differences between partners in government, notably in Bonn and Paris.

Despite the great variety of views on security matters, some encouraging trends that would have seemed improbable only a few years ago, can also be discerned. The major West European countries have displayed a willingness to improve their defence cooperation, as reflected, for instance, in the Western European Union (WEU) platform of October 1987. West Germany and France have revived the political agreements concluded in 1963 between de Gaulle and Adenauer, held common military exercises, broke the stalemate regarding the development and procurement of a modern attack helicopter and underlined their common efforts by agreeing to set up a joint Franco-German brigade. In conjunction with growing discussion about Europeanization of French security policy, the French military contribution to the defence of Western Europe has become more purposeful, and in some measure this affects more generally cooperation between French and integrated NATO forces.

Discussion between Britain and France concerning cooperation on nuclear arms and the pending Memorandum Of Understanding (MOU) on logistical support are also potentially powerful signals that the major West European countries are readjusting their defence efforts. But these steps should not be overestimated. Obstacles to Western European defence cooperation also do exist -- as do opposition parties which may assume government responsibility in the future and alter presently emerging policies.

The smaller West European countries are, understandably, hesitant in reacting to the new developments. In general, it seems that trans-Atlantic solidarity prevails over any other security arrangement, but voices are heard about a Western "two-pillar" defence organization, in which the European countries should take a more independent position *vis-à-vis* the United States. In some countries political parties of the Left are inclined to build a "European house", favouring much closer rapprochement between Eastern and Western Europe. Some aim at a disengagement of both superpowers from such a "political security" arrangement in Europe, while others go as far as incorporating the Soviet Union in it and -- implicity or explicity -- excluding the United States. The dilemmas for these countries are as acute as for the bigger European powers, but it is more the nature of smaller powers to adopt a wait-and-see attitude.

Thus a division has been created within every Western country. Given the pluralist alliance of pluralist societies it will not only be difficult to maintain the discipline needed to present the alliance as a strategic unity in global bargaining; even more so to reach a unitary view of the objectives, risks and costs involved. The necessary coherence should be the result of a process which would start from the bottom, i.e. from the recognition, articulation and conciliation of the various national perspectives, interests and priorities.

## *V. Policy Recommendations*

### 1. The Necessity of a Western European Response

Based on the complex picture emerging from the survey of Gorbachev's first three years in power, the question with which the Western European leaders are now faced is whether or not these changes warrant a "new" set of attitudes *vis-à-vis* the Soviet Union and Eastern Europe, with the resulting implications for political, trade and security relations.

A recent bi-partisan American report, for instance, argues that Gorbachev's new policies "challenge the United States and its allies to reexamine many of the assumptions behind their own policies toward the Soviet Union"; these policies demanded an "active response" by the West rather than a "purely reactive approach".[1] In many West European quarters as well, and not just on the left side of the political spectrum, the changes occurring, or said to occur, in the Soviet Union are seen as a unique opportunity to reshape fundamental issues left unresolved since the war. Combined with the deep anti-nuclear *malaise* left by ten years of Euromissile battles, the new Soviet approach, including a much more dynamic arms control and disarmament policy *vis-à-vis* Western Europe, may carry the security debate in our countries well beyond what prudence would warrant. Differences of security outlook on both sides of the Atlantic, and within Western Europe itself, may also add to the problem and ultimately threaten, perhaps irreversibly, the basic Western consensus on the Soviet Union which had been at the core of the Western security system since the end of World War II.

Hence, defining a set of policy options toward the Soviet Union and gathering the widest possible consensus around such a platform should become a matter of

1 *How should America Respond to Gorbachev's Challenge?,* A Report of the Task Force on Soviet New Thinking, Institute for East-West Security Studies, New York 1987.

top priority for Europe and the Alliance as a whole. In doing so, if one is to avoid blunders of historic proportions, based either on over-optimistic expectations (which may lead to disillusionment and disappointments) or, conversely, on merely passive attitudes (which may miss the chance of exploiting potential opportunities), it is necessary to tackle beforehand, and in as serene a fashion as possible, a number of complex and interrelated issues. What follows is an attempt to explore some of these issues, both in terms of methodology and substance.

## 2. Frame of Reference

The interrelationship between Western policy options and Soviet changes is both inescapable politically and potentially misleading if it is used as the sole determinant of our policy options. It is inescapable because much of the collective security system built after World War II was dictated by and found its public legitimacy in a common Western view of the Soviet system as basically threatening, militaristic and totalitarian, geared toward territorial and ideological expansion. In that sense, Stalin, even Khrushchev, and certainly Brezhnev, were -- as Marxists would put it -- "objective allies" of the Western security system, legitimizing our continued deterrence efforts, and helping, in fact, to maintain cohesion among our countries, inspite of ongoing societal changes and necessarily diverse historical memories.

With Gorbachev, Western democracies face, and are likely to face, a far more daunting challenge: that of maintaining and legitimizing effective armed forces and a prudent deterrent *vis-à-vis* a Soviet regime that claims that it is "radically" changing and throwing overboard its militaristic propensities of the past, dismantling brand-new intermediate-range nuclear missiles and withdrawing from Afghanistan.

Quite naturally, this is bound to encourage optimistic expectations, sometimes wild expectations, among Western public opinion, and by implication to provoke potentially dangerous divisons among our countries, and at times within the same government in a given country.

With this background, it is particularly important to avoid the danger of having our security debates dictated not in accordance with our definition as to what our interests are, but by conflicting assessments of whether or not the Soviet Union has changed, or will eventually change, its "true nature". Unfortunately, although not surprisingly, there are signs that this may already be occurring.

At one extreme, a substantial fringe of the European Left (not to speak of the environmentalist-pacifist groups) is rushing to espouse Gorbachev's vision of a disarmed, denuclearized and neutral Western Europe in the "common European house". At the other extreme, some conservative commentators insist that no changes whatsoever are taking place in the USSR, or that if they are, they were at best, cosmetic and aimed at lulling Western opinion into a dangerous illusion of security.

Both extremes, it seems, provide an equally erroneous basis for building future policy towards the Soviet Union. It is imprudent to take Gorbachev's words at face value and to sign a blank cheque mortgaging our security simply on the good intentions now proclaimed by the current Soviet leader, however enlightened he may sound or actually be. European history has, unfortunately, taught us that security cannot be built on pieces of paper alone, nor on good intentions. Moreover, no one can guarantee -- even if Mr. Gorbachev actually does genuinely desire a nuclear-free world by the year 2000 -- that his successor(s) will share his dream. And even if a nuclear-free and disarmed Europe could be constructed, this would tend to result in the kind of security system which under pre-nuclear conditions time and again has failed to prevent wars in Europe.

Similarly, the counsel to stand fast and ignore what goes on in the Soviet Union, as if changes in the largest empire and the biggest power on the Eurasian landmass were somehow unimportant, is also not an acceptable course of action. It is unacceptable, first, because the changes which are occurring in many sectors of Soviet life, as the analytical part of this Report shows, reflect tensions and a corresponding evolution within the system, and this may be used to gradually move East-West relations in Europe toward a more stable, more open relationship, and one based less on military power than in the past. Second, democracies do not have the option of condemning their peoples to a message of gloom and doom. Peaceful change -- "surmounting Yalta", as President Mitterand once put it -- has to be part of our message, given precisely the legitimate aspirations of our peoples, and the fact that we cannot, and should not, turn our societies into armed garrisons.

If neither of these extreme options, over-optimistic activism on the one hand, and political ostracism on the other, provide a reasonable basis for policy, what one is left with is a basically pragmatic approach which should integrate both a clear understanding of our goals and a set of interrelated but specific policies adapted to each sector of our relationship with the Soviet Union and its East European allies.

3. Clarity in the Pursuit of Objectives

In terms of *goals*, we should be clear about what we are trying to achieve in our relationship with the Soviet Union. Too often there seems to be a confusion between promoting our own interests, as we define them (e.g. maintaining stability and security at the lowest possible levels of armaments, while moving towards a long-term peaceful evolution of the political order in Europe in the direction of our own basic societal and human values) and the desire to "encourage" or "promote" change in the Soviet system in directions we deem more palatable to us. Hence the debate we now see emerging in our countries about how we should not only welcome, but also *help* Gorbachev's reforms, e.g. through trade or technology transfer. Implicit in this reasoning are the assumptions that: (1) Gorbachev's reforms, since they imply a "moderation" of Soviet power, basically are in our interests; (2) the "conservatives" or "hawks" in the Soviet Union who resist *perestroika* are, therefore, not only Gorbachev's opponents but our adversaries as well; (3) we have the power to help Gorbachev to "succeed" in his reforms; and (4) if we were to fail to extend help, we would miss a "historical opportunity" to fundamentally reshape the Soviet Union and our relations with that country.

Some of these assumptions are debatable. It is, for instance, by no means clear that we have the actual means to support this or that group within the Soviet apparatus. Inclinations to that effect recall traditional "Kremlinological" dilemmas in trying to identify "hawks" and "doves" in the USSR and how we ought to try to influence their relationship. It is also unclear whether an economically stronger and better run Soviet Union would be a lesser adversary than a declining and inefficient power. Certainly, Gorbachev himself has said time and again that his goal is to make the system work better rather than to dismantle it.

Nevertheless, Gorbachev's reforms do imply a moderation of the Soviet system, a lessening of the ideological antagonism and of the military-political confrontation between East and West so characteristic of most of the post-war era. To facilitate such a development has always been, and should continue to be, part of our approach to the Soviet Union. This should be valid even if Gorbachev, or some of his staunch or reluctant allies. in the party apparat, conceive of *perestroika* as some kind of "breathing space" (*peredyshka*). From Brest-Litovsk to the New Economic Policy (NEP) and the Molotov-Rippentrop Pact, there have been such pauses before. Also, there have been attempts at reform, like the ones undertaken by Malenkov and Khrushchev in the 1950s, which failed.

However, what makes the present period different from preceding ones in the fact that significant success in the modernization of the Soviet political, social and economic system (including a substantial improvement in economic performance), in Gorbachev's view and in that of most Western specialists, can be brought about only by far-reaching domestic and international "opening", political "liberalization" and "democratization" and the introduction of market principles in the economy. Such a process undoubtedly, as the Soviet party leader has made clear, will take a long time. But to expect that after several decades, or even several "generations" as he has said, the USSR would be able simply to return to ideological antagonism and military-political confrontation is unreasonable. Even if some parts of the Soviet apparatus conceive of the present stage of a "pause", there is most likely to be a dialectical interrelationship between *perestroika* and *peredyshka.* At its end could emerge a Soviet state and Soviet system which would distinguish itself substantially from the present one. It could be, as George Kennan has put it, more of a "country" than a "cause".

Thus, to try -- within the limits set to corresponding attempts -- to influence such a development should be part of our objectives. We should constructively engage the Soviet Union and not simply wait for the internal tensions in the Soviet system to bring about change. At the very least, if we cannot help along the process of change, we should not hinder it.

At the same time, we should combine constructive engagement with patience and firmness as to the defence of our own interests and values. A corresponding policy ought to be carefully calibrated according to the area in question (e.g. politics, trade and security relations) and to specific countries (i.e. the Soviet Union and/or its allies).

What follows is an effort to define some of these policies.

## 4. A Western European Policy Agenda

### a. Preserving the Balance Between Security and Other Areas

Whereas the Soviet agenda remains focused primarily on security and arms control, with trade as an important appendix but human rights almost non-existent, our own agenda and its sequence of implementation should be different. From our perspective, it should be clear that significant measures of East-West arms control, notwithstanding major alterations to the current European security regime (i.e. in the form of massive reductions of conventional or nuclear forces) should only come as the final stage of a process of gradual change which would have brought about a number of tangible results in the areas of political affairs, human rights and trade, and altered the character of Soviet-Eastern European relations.

There is a fundamental contradiction here between the slow and difficult pace of domestic economic and social changes, which Gorbachev is trying to force in the Soviet Union, and the immediate and revolutionary transformation of the security order he wants Western Europeans to accept in the form of arms control. From the perspective of our interests, the sequence of events should be exactly the opposite, both in terms of substance and the time frame. Change in the Soviet Union and Eastern Europe should be emphasized since, to build a "common European house", it is necessary to agree on its very foundation, namely, basic human rights. A careful balance between the various aspects of our relationship with the East should, therefore, remain the foremost priority in our approach.

b. Adjusting Policy to Different Time Frames

Policies should be based on the awareness that East-West relations are an *interaction process*, and careful distinctions should be made as to the different time frames involved for achieving different objectives.

In the short run, the West should welcome agreements, on economic exchanges, cultural relations and arms control, which seem in the mutual interest and help in the solution of regional conflicts like, for instance, promoting political solutions in Afghanistan after Soviet withdrawal or arranging an arms embargo in the Iraq-Iran war. While promoting such agreements, it should, on the one hand, be careful not to mistake them for the end of the East-West conflict. On the other hand, it should -- with the above mentioned qualifications as to then likely effectiveness in mind -- favor such Soviet policies as have a chance to contribute to increased openness and autonomy for Soviet and, even more so, for East European societies.

For the long run, the West should project its own version of a more peaceful, more just and freer international system. It should encourage the participation of the Soviet Union, as a full-fledged member in that system and in the full knowledge that this would mean welcoming not only a contributor to common global tasks but also a more active and difficult competitor. The West owes it to itself to accept the risks involved, as long as the competition is more peaceful and more open than today.

To the notion of the "common European house", West Europeans should respond by reaffirming at the same time:

- the legitimacy and value of the American alliance and physical presence;
- the right of Western Europe to its distinctive identity and defence, and its commitment to creating their political basis;
- the artificiality of Europe's division and the aspiration to undo it, through the "renaissance" and reinforcement of traditional human, cultural and economic

ties, and through collaboration in common tasks (e.g. in environmental matters) and through expansion of modern telecommunications.

But in the middle run, which politically and strategically may be the most relevant dimension, the West must even more than before try to counter the potentially dangerous implications of Soviet strategy and develop a strategy of its own. As always, such a response can only be essentially defensive and based on containment. But neither defence, as Gorbachev's foreign policy activism shows, nor containment are necessarily passive or static. On the contrary, Gorbachev's new approaches have to be met by much more flexible tactics than before. Even more importantly, his new emphasis on ideological competition and on arms control based on public diplomacy, on influencing collective perceptions and on playing upon social forces, make it imperative for the West to realize that the prime task of strategy today is political. As important as deterrence and defence is the peace-time struggle for the minds of men, in the West and in the East, notably in Europe -- and even more specifically in Central Europe.

c. Coordinating Western Policies

Eloquent analyses exist in the West which have documented the sorry state in which divergent and contradictory policies have brought the alliance. They have outlined a basic choice between pragmatism aimed at perpetuating a crumbling status quo and a long range, coherent strategy aimed at modifying the behavior of the Warsaw Pact. From this, recommendations have been derived for a comprehensive plan for arms control in Europe, but which would be part of a broader strategy aimed at inducing Soviet military self-restraint through economic incentives.

While this integrated conception should serve as a "regulatory idea" in the Kantian sense, i.e. as an inspiration for the direction in which various policies should converge, it is clear that, the need for Western unity and for linkage notwithstanding, actual policies will depend upon specific interests and contexts. Given a pluralist alliance of pluralist societies it would not only be difficult to keep the discipline needed to maintain the conditionality necessary for global bargaining, but even more so to reach a unitary view of objectives, the risks and the costs involved. Even on the Eastern side, whatever the centraliszation of the empire and the flexibility at the top, it is probably not in Gorbachev's power to deliver his side of any Grand Deal.

This is not, however, a prescription for accepting the present cacophony. Rather, as mentioned, the necessary -- if necessarily imperfect -- coherence should be seen as the result of a process which would start from the bottom, i.e. from the recognition, articulation and conciliation of the various perspectives, interests and priorities, national and transnational, which have emerged in recent years and have led to the well-known clashes on sanctions, on technology transfer, or on missile deployment and withdrawals.

Between the desirable comprehensive and coherent strategy for the West and the multiple ties and divisions created by cultural traditions, geopolitical situations or economic interests, some bridges are needed, of which a West European point of view is probably the most natural. Precisely because Gorbachev seems to be a master in the old Soviet game of playing off Americans and Europeans, nuclear and non-nuclear proponents, Germans and French, left and right, against each other, the articulation of a conception of European perspectives and interests would be extremely useful as a guide to the actual dialogues going on between various Western and Eastern partners.

d. Integrating European Security and Arms Control

For Western European liberal democracies, sustaining a continuing military competition is an unnatural condition. Western Europe's strength, internally and in its relations with the Soviet Union and Eastern Europe, results from its political liberties and economic prosperity. In the Soviet perspective this has always been the dominant challenge. While the on-going military competition is fueled by many sources on either side of the divide, it has often served Soviet interests, has deflected Western political penetration of Eastern Europe and, conversely, provided the one currency for Soviet influence in Western Europe.

Despite some new inflections in theory, the Soviet Union has continued to deny Western security interests in practice and has rejected Western notions of common security which have evolved since the late 1950s. These notions do require a measure of military self-restraint. Instead, successive Soviet leaderships, since the early 1960s, have made a steady effort to strengthen military power and to instrumentalise it politically. They have done so through attempts at progressive denial of NATO response options and removal of the American protective umbrella from Western Europe, and notably from the Federal Republic. By means of, as Evgenii Primakov called it, a "dialectics of interaction" between Soviet military power and Western public opinion, Moscow has attempted to gain acceptance for *its* concept of European security.

For Western Europe the choices are between

- staying in the military competition with the hope for an eventual change of its boundary conditions;
- accomodation in the hope of Soviet moderation;

- pursuit of a competitive political strategy which would offer incentives for Soviet military self-restraint and remove military power from the central place it has occupied in East-West relations.

The Harmel doctrine was designed to provide for such a strategy. However, its promise was not fulfilled as primacy was given to detente and arms control at the expense of defence. This resulted in a political stalemate with a modest momentum of change, which either side could interpret in its favour: the Soviet Union in terms of the military balance, and the West in terms of political penetration of Eastern Europe.

More recently, and particularly since the Gorbachev's advent to power, the European agenda is beginning to change. Of course, his efforts can only in the medium and long term be expected to produce Soviet self-restraint and less competitive policies towards the West. But it is only the kind of reforms he envisages which contain the promise for the West that it may be able to escape from its present security predicaments.

This leaves Western Europe with a new kind of political dilemma. While it would be in its interest to withhold changes in the basic military security structure until the political underpinnings for a new structure have evolved, little will probably result from change in the Soviet Union without some degree of Western responsiveness to what is conceived to be a more constructive Soviet approach to arms control. Responsiveness would tend to stabilize Soviet policies of reform; conversely, lack of responsiveness would hardly be acceptable among Western publics. This situation is worsened by the fact that the Soviet Union has abundant negotiating leverage, whereas Western European public opinion will press for ever more reductions, and perhaps ever more "zero solutions", although NATO is reaching certain limits beyond which it will no longer be able to implement a sound strategy of deterrence. Precisely for the reason that, for most Western Europeans, the on-going East-West competition is regarded as political in nature, they will tend to look for an approach that may disregard military realities.

Under these circumstances, agreement should be reached on a number of conceptual issues.

- As the Soviet Union has regained the diplomatic and political initiative in the arms control and disarmament arena since the early 1980s, it is necessary for Western Europe to react with the reaffirmation that the basic features of the Atlantic Alliance are not going to be subject to East-West negotiation. This should extend to both the principle of Western security cooperation and to the continued importance of deterrence.

- Soviet arms control plus "public diplomacy", as well as Soviet military build-ups, have apparently been governed by a long term concept of European security, wheras Western arms control policies have increasingly been determined by domestic politics. To shape eventual outcomes in its favour, Western Europe needs to entertain some notion of what kind of European security structure it would prefer if the existing one were to be replaced. Such a notion would have to relate to both the definition of deterrence and the design of negotiations with the Warsaw Pact countries. Deterrence and disarmament (negotiations) need to be explained in terms of their political nature; changing either would mean to change the existing security order.

- It has become commonplace to explain the political nature of arms control and defence policies in terms of the Harmel doctrine. However, as mentioned, a reversal of that doctrine seems to have occurred. Originally, the doctrine provided for defence and military security as a *precondition* for political normalization; arms control was regarded as a *subordinate* means to regulate the continuing arms competition and to facilitate change. In the application of the doctrine since the mid-1970s, however, arms control has acquired primacy over defence and has become largely identified with political normalization. Of course, current Soviet reforms call for a Western political strategy; but rather than asking for a second phase of the revised Harmel doctrine, Western Europe should restore its original meaning -- with one important addition. The original Harmel report (except for declaring political normalization a policy goal) failed to define long-term, structural objectives; the new doctrine should formulate such a set of objectives.

- The Soviet Union never explicitly accepted the principle of nuclear deterrence as a political doctrine confining the application of military power to the avoidance or termination of war. She continued instead to entertain a traditional notion of using military forces for political objectives, and one that was not inherently governed by self-restraint. She also seems to have assumed that nuclear deterrence could falter despite the massive stockpiles remaining in place. Thus, dismantling nuclear deterrence in the West could, in the Soviet view, remove a nuclear shadow cast over the existence of the USSR. At the same time, such changes could restore conventional military options. For whatever the prospects of political change in the Soviet Union, force structure trends have been in the direction of a Soviet capacity for a conventional war; in the judgment of many Western military analysts, she could terminate such a war on her terms. If such an option existed, it would enable the Warsaw Pact to isolate a country like the Federal Republic strategically. A constructive Western European approach to disarmament, therefore, must not jeopardize nuclear deterrence, which ought to remain valid even under conditions of enhanced conventional stability; furthermore, it must be oriented toward reducing Soviet confidence in possibly being able to terminate conventional war on Soviet terms.

- In Soviet diplomacy, since the 1960s, priority has been given to nuclear over conventional arms control, and this is likely to continue. This leads to a Western dilemma. On the one hand, postponing nuclear arms control until conventional stability has been achieved would simply produce another stalemate and more frustration domestically in the Western European countries. On the other hand, a comprehensive negotiating approach, combining nuclear and conventional arms control talks, has never been tried since the Zorin-McCloy negotiations in 1961; its possible repetition has clearly been rejected by the Alliance, most outspokenly by France. However, the Soviet approach to "dual capable systems" -- the proposal to include all systems capable of carrying nuclear weapons, though not the warheads themselves, in conventional stability talks -- shows that the Soviet Union is guided by a comprehensive negotiating concept. Obstacles to internal agreement notwithstanding, NATO needs to be guided by some comprehensive concept of its own, relating negotiations to objectives, and partial negotiations to each other, as well as implementing stages of one agreement in conjunction with clearly specified provisions of another.

While the West, and Western Europe in particular, will have to engage in an intensive process of arms control negotiations, it will no longer be in a situation in which compatibility of arms control negotiations and strategy can be taken as given. Unlike in past experience, the very concept and the implementation of deterrence strategy have begun to change in unpredictable directions, and the only way to restore deterrence strategy in view of the momentum of arms control diplomacy is to define strategic requirements in their own right. This will require adoption of a dual approach which would differ from the double-track model in that it would (1) commit NATO to defence planning as measured by *military* requirements and (2) make clear to the Soviet leaders that their military policies will affect NATO defence planning at specified thresholds but (3) that would also have in place fallback positions if, either unilaterally or in bilateral or multilateral negotiations, Soviet military self-restraint were to materialize.

A Western European approach following these guidelines may not suffice to deflect political pressures towards premature arms control agreements nor remove obstacles on the road toward force modernization. But it would be the only way to persuade the Soviet leaders that, without downgrading the political role of Soviet military power on the European continent, it will not be possible to establish a stable European order that would help resolve internal problems on either side of the systemic divide. The consequences which arise from the above guidelines for arms control negotiations, as well as force planning, can be stated as follows:

- A *START Agreement* deserves Western European support because it could help stabilize the superpower relationship. However, Western Europe should guard against excessive Soviet-American bilateralism at the expense of European security. In particular, it should reject any agreement (e.g. on nuclear-armed, sea-launched cruise missiles) that could deprive NATO even further of the means for selective employment options and thus of extended deterrence.

- On the European arms control agenda, high priority should be given to *conventional stability talks*. Reduction of the Soviet invasion capability and denial of the option for high-confidence, short-preparation-time attack should be made the litmus test for Soviet "new thinking" on European security. However, even if there were to be an agreement on conventional arms control, providing force stability at lower levels of armament, nuclear deterrence would remain an essential prerequisite for European security.

- *Nuclear arms control* in Europe should be governed by redefined nuclear force requirements for continued deterrence, and it should be contingent on progress in conventional arms control. While theatre nuclear force structure developments in the Alliance have to provide for a restucturing of short-range nuclear forces (follow-on to Lance) and credible means for longer range options (e.g. stand-off and nuclear capable sea- and air-launched cruise missiles), such developments could allow for unilateral reductions of warheads and, possibly, negotiated ceilings for short-range nuclear missiles.

- The removal of *chemical weapons* of NATO and the Warsaw Pact under an adequately verifiable and comprehensive agreement would clearly be in NATO's favour. (See, for instance, the joint ESG / Aspen Strategy Group Report of 1986.) However, the obstacles on the road to a comprehensive agreement are still considerable, and the implications of a regional agreement for the most part undesirable for all the NATO countries.

- The *CSCE/CDE process* is unlikely to generate substantial constraints on usable military power in Europe. But this forum is becoming increasingly important as a stage in which some all-European framework of security will be shaped. To that extent, Western European interest should pertain particularly to the creation of a relationship between the Soviet Union and Eastern Europe, based on a more equal status, and one that would facilitate more cooperative relations between Eastern and Western Europe and contribute to more transparency and confidence-building in military affairs. In this context Soviet proposals for naval measures should be weigh carefully in regard to both stabilizing effects and constraints on US support.

- The Soviet offers of exchanging data on conventional forces and military expenditures should be followed up. If pursued vigorously, the process would show the realities as they are: that the Soviet armed forces are superior is almost in every category of weapons and in ground and air forces in Central Europe, and that the Soviet Union spends a significantly higher proportion on defence as a proportion of the gross nation produce (GNP) than the NATO countries. Western failure to respond would threaten to undermine even further the public support in NATO countries for defence programmes help the Soviet leadership retain the diplomatic initiative, and weaken those civilian forces in the USSR as are interested in promoting military *glasnost* as well as pluralizing access to national security information.

e. Promotion of Human Rights

Respect for human rights and fundamental freedoms is an essential factor for European security. It is also to be regarded as the very foundation of any "common European house". In this respect, the West should invoke the comprehensive framework of the CSCE Final Act, the provisions of which have lost none of their topicality and importance. They include such *desiderata* as facilitation of freer movement and contacts, individually and collectively, whether privately or officially, among persons institutions and organizations of the CSCE participant states; expansion of contacts and regular meetings on the basis of family ties; reunification of families; travel for personal or professional reasons; improvement of conditions for tourism on an individual or collective basis; meetings among young people; broadening of the existing links and cooperation in the field of sports; improvement of the circulation of, access to, and exchange of information; the creation of better working conditions for journalists; and the strengthening of ties in cultural matters and the field of education.

Of course, it was under Brezhnev that the Soviet Union agreed to such principles, and one of the problems since then has been that they have not sufficiently been put in practice. Today, however, new conditions obtain. As the Analysis shows, the Soviet leadership under Gorbachev itself considers "modernization" of the Soviet economy and the Soviet system to be impossible if it remained confined to administrative and technocratic measures. It has recognised that a modern, efficient economy depends on inidiviual initiative, voluntary cooperation and a better "quality of life" and, therefore, on some political pluralism, more room for autonomous social acitivity, the introduction of market elements in the economy and more international communication and exchanges.

This trend should be actively encouraged. However, too public and too rigid a "linkage" of "progress" on human rights in the USSR with Western economic and political "concessions", probably hinders rather than helps the reformist impetus. What is required is adopting a sensible course between, on the one hand, unacceptable disinterest in how the Soviet authorities treat their citizenry and, on the other, vociferous campaigns conducted with the aim of changing the Soviet system.

Such a middle course has, for quite some time, been practised successfully by the Federal Republic *vis-à-vis* the the Soviet Union in its attempt to improve the living conditions of the ethnic Germans in the USSR and to better their possibilities for emigration. (The relations of the Federal Republic with the GDR would be another case in point.) The West German approach has consisted in pointing to what could be called "objective" linkages; namely, that Soviet (and, respectively, East German) moves on the question of human and civil rights will lead to a different framework of relations in which the *economic* benefits, which are seen as so important in the East, have a much better chance of being realised.

f. Expanding Economic Exchanges

Since policy recommendations on economic matters, as on any other, should not primarily be formulated under the aspect of what is desirable, but of what is *possible*, such recommendations have to be based on the following three premises.

First, the most important guarantee for economic reform in the Soviet Union may be the lack of a realistic alternative; the most important retarding factor may be the inability of political and economic actors, and the society as a whole, to accept and absorb new ideas. There is, therefore, no plausible reason to assume that the reform process in the Soviet Union will advance at a faster rate than in Hungary, where it was started in 1968 and where it has taken almost two decades for some elements of interdependence with the world economy to become effective.

Second, even if the West were to grant large sums of credit and deliver a substantial volume of technology, the impact of Western economic measures on the Soviet system should be regarded as marginal. In the near future the Soviet system will not be flexible enough to absorb Western assistance and to use it, in more than an incremental fashion, for the modernization of the economy. The low degree of integration of the Soviet economy into the world market is not only one of its weaknesses but, in Soviet eyes, also one of its strengths: Denial of trade does not provide the West with much leverage.

Third, even given the best of Soviet efforts at modernization, there is no realistic prospect for a fast expansion of trade and economic cooperation with the West. Hence, what is necessary in the short and medium term for Gorbachev's "restructuring" to be reasonably successful is some cooperative effort on the Western part, some change in the terms of trade (price increases for oil and natural gas) and much effort on the Soviet side simply to arrest the recent trend (in terms of trade flows) of a further disassociation of the Soviet economy from the world market.

On the basis of these premises the following recommendations can be made:

- The Soviet leaders should be asked to enter into a dialogue on a framework for economic interdependence between East and West. The main "contribution" to this dialogue they have made so far is to blame the West for protectionism in trade and the Coordinating Committee for Trade with Communist Countries (Cocom) for its restrictions (which, indeed, are another form of protectionism). They have made only very few *constructive* proposals for a system of interdependence. To be listed among them are the ideas for an all-European free trade zone. But this notion has been defined, since the early 1950s, as a model for integration among market-type economies. The dialogue, therefore, should first lead to an elaboration of the indispensible elements of a free trade zone and a clarification as to the extent to which, and in what form, the socialist countries are prepared to accept them. Certainly, as only the first steps on a long journey towards a new network of communication and exchanges have been taken by the Soviet Union, any talk about membership in the European Community is, to say the least, premature.

- Participation of the Soviet Union in international economic organizations should not be made an end in itself. The admission of the Soviet Union to GATT and the IMF would not automatically lead to changes in the domestic economic system, and assurances by the Soviet leaders that they are prepared to play by the rules of the (world) market economy at this stage are not very convincing. What is called for is for the West to indicate that, in principle, these organizations are open to the Soviet Union but that significant domestic and foreign trade reform measures are necessary first to make Soviet assurances appear credible.

- The Western industrialized countries should help the Soviet reform effort by offering credit and technology but only if this is in the Western economic interest. Subsidies are politically controversial and generally should be avoided. The same should apply to joint ventures, which are at the moment high on the list of Soviet priorities for economic cooperation with the West. Western governments should perhaps encourage but not force the pace on that issue and leave it up to the individual firms concerned as to whether or not they consider such schemes to be in their own interest.

- The extension of know-how for an efficient, decentralized and competitive system operating in an open society should be regarded as particularly fruitful. Offers could be made for management training. Soviet university students and management personnel, when returning to the USSR, could promote much flexibility and interdependence with the West even without necessarily, or initially, touching the essence of the system. This should be in Gorbachev's, as well as in the Western, interest.

g. Encouraging Eastern European Emancipation

Given the state of affairs in Eastern Europe, what attitudes and practical policies can Western Europe adopt towards the communist states and societies in the Eastern part of the continent?

Assuming that "reform is good" both for the people in the countries that practise it, and for the East-West relationship in general, Western Europe should cooperate more closely with regimes which proceed with reforms in earnest, or wish to initiate them, than with those which reject reformism or pay only lip service to the concept of change. Perhaps some more direct influence in a direction desirable from the Western point of view can be exerted on the East European countries than on the Soviet Union.

As Eastern Europe remains diverse, the Western policy of "differentiation" should continue. Emancipation from Soviet tutelage has, nevertheless, ceased to be the main criterion according to which an Eastern European country can be judged "better" than others. (Romania, for example, is now "emancipating" itself from a reformist program that would benefit its people but is no longer disturbing the Soviet Union's foreign political and military programmes to any meaningful extent.) The two new criteria for a differentiated approach by the West are serious reforms of the economy and relaxation of domestic repression.

East-West European economic and technological interaction is and will remain limited. Reform has not yet made, and will not make for a long time, the communist regimes of Europe more competitive and more economically compatible with Western systems. No large schemes of capitalist assistance to communist modernization (like the one that Poland attempted in the first half of the 1970s) can and should be entertained. Also, by and large, subsidies should be avoided since they tend to hinder rather than help market-oriented reforms.

Within these limits, a measured and friendly economic cooperation can develop. While loans and credits should be governed by normal economic criteria, Western European governments, companies and community institutions should look favourably at small and intermediate Eastern European modernization *desiderata*, but not at grand state-wide programs. Economic interaction between East and West Germany will evidently constitute a special case, not quite following the patterns elsewhere in Eastern Europe.

Hungary, too, is a special case. The survival of Hungarian reforms appears of some importance for the fate of reforms everywhere in the bloc, including the USSR. Should the Hungarian experiment collapse or slide down very badly, both Gorbachev and the Eastern European reform-anxious constituencies would suffer a serious setback; conversely, the conservative factions would benefit. If at all possible, Western Europe should devise a "save the Hungarian reforms" economic plan and implement it in cooperation with the Hungarian leadership. This may require ingeniousness beyond the usual give-them-money attitude.

West European economic assistance to environmental protection in Eastern Europe is highly commendable not only for its practical effect but also because of the psychological impact it has on the recipients. It should be widely popularized. Similarly, targeting preferential economic activity on some of the abysmally failing social areas would have an auspicious effect on the Eastern European publics. Helping people, as it were, rather than bailing out failed regimes, would upgrade the West European image. This could perhaps be achieved by cooperative schemes such as West European economic participation in the Eastern European health services; the building of hospitals and pharmaceutical plants; special terms for the purchase of state-of-art medical equipment; cooperative East-West housing construction projects; and contribution to the expansion of educational facilities.

Human rights and cultural freedom in Eastern Europe should also remain a major West European concern. Reintegration into official reformism of persons ostracized for political reasons (Solidarity in Poland; Charter 77 in Czechoslovakia; publication of banned writers, etc.) is one of the avenues to be pursued. The time may have come when the Eastern European governments will accept more extensive Western cultural presence. This may include cultural institutes; language-teaching facilities with Western participation; more frequent film weeks; and television "bridges," as already practised between Austria and Hungary and as the Soviets and the Americans have commenced to launch.

While being cooperative in the economic and cultural fields, Western Europe can well afford to stand firm on matters of principle. Among other things, the Gorbachevian theme of the singularity of a "European House" common to all (which has been echoed by others, like Erich Honecker and even Vasil Bilak) should be exposed for the disingenuous slogan that it is for the time being. Europeanism "from the Atlantic to the Urals" is an intrinsic part of the civilization which Western Europe has never ceased to cherish. But it cannot represent a practical political platform as long as the other side does not respect its fundamental ingredients.

According to the Soviet argument, Europeanism is to be viewed almost exclusively in terms of territorial togetherness, non-belligerent neighbourliness, and similarity of daily habits. For the West Europeans, on the other hand, the concept is above all axiological. Not only does it entail the currents of Antiquity, Judaeo-Christian heritage, Renaissance, Reformation, and Enlightment, to which communists at best only pay lip service, and most of which they repress to this day, but also the internalization of democracy and freedom as an inherent European experience which Moscow continues to defy. Western Europe has already delivered the goods: West Germany is living proof of the greatest reform from totalitarism to democracy so far, and the examples of Greece, Spain and Portugal should also not be lost sight of. Eastern Europe must yet show that it, too, can make Europeanism work.

# Part Two:

# Analysis

*I. Introduction*

Since his rise to power in March 1985 Gorbachev has called for a basic "restructuring" (*perestroika*) of the socio-economic and political order in the Soviet Union. He has emphasized the urgent need for a "sharp turn" in the course of events, for "major reform", -- even for a "revolution". He has demanded greater initiative, more participation and broader "democratisation", and "openness" (*glasnost*) in politics and society. In the economy he has been pressing for modernization, the faster utilisatiton of science and technology, computerisation, and a drastic improvement in performance and international competitiveness. In the military realm he has embarked on major changes in personnel, demanded greater economising and launched a debate about doctrine.

Such calls for change, and change itself, in the domestic sphere find their counterpart in Soviet foreign policy. "New thinking" in international relations has been required not only of adversaries but also of the international department of the Soviet communist party's Central Committee, the foreign ministry officials and the academic specialists at the various institutes for international affairs under the USSR Academy of Sciences. But not just new thinking has been demanded and can be observed. Soviet foreign policy behavior, too, has become more flexible. A major arms control agreement has been signed with the United States. Appeals to Europe are being made under the slogan of "our common house". There is less inclination for "adventurism" in the Third World. But there is more interest in an international division of labour in economic affairs.

Gorbachev has also stressed the close interrelationship between the Soviet domestic reform process and international affairs.

The present analysis is to provide an assessment of such interrelationships. Its aim is not to produce a comprehensive review of all aspects of change. Its objective is rather to look at Soviet domestic political, economic, social, and ideological developments, as well as structural, systemic transformations, with a view to their likely impact on the power base of the Soviet Union, and the country's ability and political will to conduct foreign policy.

"Power base" is understood to include not just the military capabilities of the Soviet Union -- even though these are important and require analysis. It is recognized that power derives from broader sources which include political stability, effective leadership, economic efficiency, scientific-technological innovation, adaptability of society, and ideological coherence.

All of these aspects are interrelated. Hence it is necessary to conduct a thorough diagnosis both of the ills afflicting the Soviet body politic and the remedies prescribed by Gorbachev to overcome them, as well as of the impact which external influences, including Western strategies, may have on the chances for improvement.

In this Analysis the following questions are considered to be of primary analytical relevance with particularly far-reaching significance for Western policy and strategy:

- Is it possible to discern trends for the curtailment of the privileged role of the armed forces in politics and society, of the priority for the military sector in the economy, and of military power in Soviet foreign policy?
- Is the slow-down in economic growth attributable to the heavy burden of military expenditures? Are the reduction in the growth rate of military outlays (in constant prices) since the mid-1970s, the renewed interest in arms control, the calls for a new military doctrine and posture, and the more cooperative stance of the Soviet Union in world affairs the result of economic constraints?
- What are the chances that Gorbachev will succeed with his policy of modernization? Does he have the right kind of domestic political backing or will he most likely, if he continues to press for major reform, end up like Khrushchev? If Gorbachev were to prevail, would he or his successor(s) -- after the current "breathing spell" -- return to the traditional, hard-line and antagonistic, stance in international politics?
- Finally, what are the differences in internal development and foreign policy of the Eastern European countries as compared to the USSR, and to what extent do they matter? What, if any, are the specific interests which Europeans may have in Soviet domestic and foreign policy change? What, if any, is the likely impact which Western European strategies can have on developments in Eastern Europe and the Soviet Union, and on the Soviet-American relationship?

The problems outlined have been addressed as follows. The impetus and primary justification of change in the Soviet Union will be considered first (ch. II). The main rationale of the intended "sharp turn" clearly lie in what Gorbachev has called "precrisis" conditions, and in the inadequate and worsening performance of the Soviet economy in the East-West competition (sect. 1). This is why this analysis begins with a discussion of economic affairs. According to its results the major effort of the reform programme does not (yet) aim at establishing a socialist market system but is still devoted to the reordering of priorities within the existing system, stepping up of pressures, and the replacement in personnel to improve performance (sect. 2), as well as to some reorganization (sect. 3). The measures taken thus far are unlikely to have much impact on economic performance; the more important of them are not even to take effect before 1991. Also foreign trade (sect. 4) is unlikely to provide much of a stimulus. Hence improvement in economic performance will most likely depend on more radical reform measures, the section concludes.

The analysis next features, within the overall economic context, a detailed discussion concerning the role of the military sector in the economy (ch. III). This includes estimates of previous and current trends in, and the burden of, defence spending (sect. 1), as well as the likelihood and consequences of cuts (sect. 2). There was considerable discussion among the members of the drafting committee as to the possible effects of savings. The view emerged as a common denominator that savings from equipment cutbacks are potentially most important. While it would probably be wrong to believe, the argument continues, that Gorbachev is being "forced" into arms control agreements by economic stringencies, the latter do provide an incentive for the former. Certainly it must be in the party leader's interest to avoid an acceleration of the arms competition.

Another important aspect scrutinized in this context is the question as to whether the military most likely supports or opposes the "restructuring" in the military and civilian economic sectors (sect. 3). To the extent that *perestroika* can enhance modernization it is being supported by the military. They may for that very reason well be prepared to accept a temporary shift in priorities. But they would expect to see, in the medium run, the effects of this switch in terms of better weapons, and a more efficient relationship between the military and the civilian sector of the economy.

This discussion provides the transition to the next chapter (ch. IV) which deals with Soviet domestic politics under Gorbachev. The nature and extent of Gorbachev's power and authority form its major focus (sect. 2). It is argued here that major impediments to fundamental change do exist but that, for the time being, there is no alternative to Gorbachev's reform effort. Major differences in the leadership are, at present, concerned with the speed and direction of the changes rather than with the principle of change itself. But domestic conflict and controversy are likely to increase as the pace of reform quickens. This also concerns civil-military relations (sect. 4). At present Gorbachev's room of manoeuvre is not so severely circumscribed by military opposition that any attempt the reordering priorities in politics, economics, and doctrine will fail. Basically the primacy of the party over the military remains unimpaired. But in this relationship, too, conflict is likely to sharpen if current tendencies of reduction in the privileged role of the armed forces in politics and society were to continue.

The discussion of Soviet foreign policy (ch. V) begins with an assessment of the changes in ideology -- "peaceful coexistence" -- and in the concepts of international relations (sect. 1). The processes of reinterpretation are regarded as moving into a, from the Western perspective, favorable direction. Less dogmatism and orthodoxy, more flexibility and cooperation are its primary ingredients. Yet these trends in ideological adaptation are incomplete and, at times, opposed by traditionalists.

The actual or incipient changes in Soviet foreign policy practice are dealt with next. Personnel changes and shifts in priorities (sect. 2), functional aspects (arms control: sect. 5) and regional problems (the Soviet Union's relationship with Eastern and Western Europe, and the United States: sect. 3 and 4) are the main subject matters under review here. From this review emerges the conclusion that Soviet foreign policy practice, just like the theory underlying it, is still in a state of flux. There are many contradictory trends. Undoubted, however, is the new degree of flexibility and the new challenges which it puts to the West.

The final chapter (ch. VI) evaluates these challenges and the response to be made primarily by the Western Europeans but also by the West as a whole. Evidently the changes in the Soviet Union have already affected Western perceptions (sect. 1), and they have given rise to both dangers and opportunities (sect. 2). As for the specific contribution Western Europe should make it is argued in the paper that this could consist in changing the currently rather narrow focus on military security and arms control, and insisting that more emphasis be given to new forms of economic cooperation, joint efforts in environmental protection, and expansion of human rights and contacts across the ideological divide.

## *II. The Soviet Economy: From Stagnation to Modernization?*

### 1. The Rationale of Gorbachev's Economic Policy

Three months before entering office as General Secretary of the CPSU, Gorbachev pointed out: "Only an intensive economy developing on the foundation of the newest science and technology can serve as a reliable basis for raising the well-being of the workers, and can assure the strengthening of the country's position in the world arena; only an intensive economy will permit it to enter the new millenium with dignity as a prosperous major power."[2]

2 At a conference of the CPSU on ideological problems, *Izvestiya*, December 12, 1984.

These by now famous words, which attracted attention not only because of their content but also because of their unideological rhetoric, unambiguously gave economic development the highest priority in the urgent need for change. They made clear beyond doubt that economic development would not be an end in itself but the prerequisite for prosperity and military strength. In face of the poor economic performance of the preceding years, when the growth of overall production had fallen to unprecedentedly low levels, the validity of Gorbachev's "economy first" could hardly be disputed.

In May 1985 he also said that the "future of socialism in the world" depended on its economic success, and that "calculations" showed that Soviet economic growth had to be at least 1 percent faster per year than it had recently been. In terms of the official Soviet figures, that meant at least 4 percent a year. The US Central Intelligence Agency's assessment of Soviet real GNP growth in 1984 (at 1982 factor cost) was 1.5 percent, so Gorbachev could be interpreted as setting a minimum politically acceptable growth rate that was, in Western terms, around 2.5 percent -- modest, and roughly equivalent to recent US growth. His speeches, and the subsequently published plan targets suggest that he was thinking of this minimum improvement as something required urgently, preferably the day after his speech, with a greater acceleration to come later on, beginning around 1990. In June 1985, in a major speech on technology policy, Gorbachev clarified that the acceleration of technological change (faster introduction and diffusion of new products and processes) was in his view the main requirement.

The background to these propositions is worth sketching in. Notoriously, Soviet economic growth had tended to slow down since the late 1950s, and especially since the mid-1970s (see Table 1).

The official Soviet statistical annual had shown Soviet national income (Soviet definition) as the same proportion of US national income, namely 67 percent, since 1975. Catching up with and overtaking the United States had officially ceased. Yet several years ago the Institute of World Economy and International Relations (IMEMO) in Moscow did make an effort to calculate the Soviet to US national income ratio (there was no report on whether Western or Soviet national income definitions were used). The estimate put Soviet production at only *half* of the American volume and indicated that the gap was widening rather than narrowing. In late 1987 the IMEMO journal published an estimate that put Soviet industrial output in 1986 at only a half of US industrial output, instead of the four-fifths ratio given in the annual statistical handbook. Claims have been made at IMEMO that such calculations have influenced policy under the present leadership.

*Table 1 - Soviet Economic Growth Since 1965*

| | 1966-70 | 1971-75 | 1976-80 | 1981-85 | 1985 | 1986 | 1987 |
|---|---|---|---|---|---|---|---|
| **A. Soviet official measures** | | | | | | | |
| NMP produced | 7.7 | 5.7 | 4.2 | 3.5 | 3.5[a] | 4.1[a] | 2.3 |
| NMP utilised | 7.1 | 5.1 | 3.9 | 3.2 | 3.1[a] | 3.6[a] | |
| Gross industrial output | 8.5 | 7.4 | 4.4 | 3.6 | 3.9 | 4.9 | 3.8 |
| Gross agricultural output[b] | 3.9 | 2.4 | 1.7 | 1.1 | 0.0 | 5.1 | 0.2 |
| Investment[b] | 7.4 | 7.2 | 5.2 | 3.2 | 3.0 | 8.0 | 4.7 |
| Capital stock | 7.5 | 7.9 | 6.8 | 6.0 | 5.5 | 5.3 | |
| Electric power | 7.9 | 7.0 | 4.5 | 3.6 | 3.5 | 3.6 | 4.1 |
| Oil, coal and gas | 5.2 | 5.4 | 4.2 | 2.5 | 2.4 | 4.6 | 3.1 |
| **B. CIA estimates[c]** | | | | | | | |
| GNP | 5.1 | 3.0 | 2.3 | 1.9 | 0.8 | 3.8 | |
| Industrial output | 6.4 | 5.5 | 2.7 | 1.9 | 2.0 | 3.1 | |
| Agricultural output | 3.6 | - 0.6 | 0.8 | 2.1 | - 1.7 | 7.3 | |
| Investment | 5.5 | 4.3 | 4.3 | 3.4 | 2.1 | 6.0 | |
| Capital stock | 7.4 | 8.0 | 6.9 | 6.2 | 5.8 | 5.5 | |
| Labour (man-hours) | 2.0 | 1.7 | 1.2 | 0.7 | 0.4 | 0.4 | |

*Notes*. General: All output series, and the investment and capital stock series are, in principle, in constant prices, i.e. they denote "real" changes. The Soviet official series, however, are known to contain an element of hidden inflation and therefore are upward biased. See also note a.

a: Soviet reported growth rates for 1985 and 1986 are more than usually upward biased. See Philip Hanson, RL Research Report, No. 76/87, February 26, 1987 and Jan Vanous in PlanEcon Report, February 11, 1987.

b: For five-year periods, the growth rates shown are those between the total for the period and the total for the preceding five-year period.

c: At 1982 ruble factor cost. 1986 figures are preliminary.

*Sources*: *Narodnoe khozyaistvo SSSR* (various years); *Pravda*, January 24, 1988; CIA, *Handbook of Economic Statistics 1986*; CIA and DIA, *Gorbachev's Modernization Program: A Status Report*, Paper prepared for the Subcommittee on Secuirty Economics of the US Congress Joint Economic Committee, March 19, 1987.

There is no need to dwell on the Soviet leaders' reasons for being concerned about slow growth. Military competition, international prestige and the containing of domestic discontent are all at issue. Thus, they must regard the current fad in Washington of worrying about American competitiveness as a joke in rather poor taste. According to an American journalist, a Central Committee lecturer recently told a Moscow audience that if Soviet technological capabilities could not be rapidly improved the USSR would lose military parity with the USA in 5-7 years, and that if *perestroika* failed there "would not be socialism" in the Soviet Union in the year 2000.[3] (He evidently expected his audience to be alarmed, not overjoyed, by this prospect.) It is worth bearing in mind, moreover, that the leaders' sense of urgency must have been sharpened by two other considerations. First, labour and capital input growth is virtually doomed to slow further through 1990, and natural-resource exploitation costs are likely to go on rising. Second, a mere extrapolation of past trends into the future would lead to zero and then negative growth.

Whatever the case may be with past projections, it is current economic policies which matter. These can be considered under three headings. First, policy in the narrow sense, i.e. resource allocation priorities, personnel changes, and the degree of pressure exerted by the central authorities on lower levels of the economic hierarchy. Second, reorganization (which is not necessarily "reform" in the usual sense of market reform), meaning the introduction of significant changes in economic institutions and procedures. Third, the approach to economic relations with the rest of the world.

## 2. Priorities, Pressure, Personnel

The priority changes can be very briefly summarized as follows. In accordance with Gorbachev's demands for "radical reforms" and "restructuring" of the whole society, "acceleration" of economic growth is the main objective of the Five Year Plan 1986-1990 and modernization of productive assets its cornerstone. The share of investment in national income is supposed to rise, the share of the engineering sector in investment is also to rise (at the expense, very broadly, of the consumer sector and social infrastructure but not at the expense of the energy sector and chemicals). No doubt, the plan is setting ambitious targets as the following figures demonstrate:

3 Antero Pietila, *The Baltimore Sun*, June 2, 1987.

*Table 2 - Annual Growth Rates of Production, Investment, and Consumer Satisfaction Indices*

| | 1981-85 (achieved) | 1986-90 (planned) | 1986 (achieved) | 1987 (achieved) |
|---|---|---|---|---|
| NMP (produced) | 3.5 | 4.2 | 4.1 | 2.3 |
| Industry | 3.6 | 4.6 | 4.9 | 3.8 |
| Machine-building | 6.2 | 7.4 | 6.0 | 4.6 |
| Agriculture | 1.1* | 2.7* | 5.1 | 0.2 |
| Total investment | 3.2 | 4.3* | 8.0 | 4.7 |
| Investment in machine-building | 3.2 | 12.5 | 6.0 | |
| Wages in state sector | 2.4 | 2.8 | 2.7 | 2.8 |
| Retail trade turnover | 4.0 | 5.9** | 7.1** | |

*Notes*:
* growth of five years' sum over preceding five years' sum
** excluding sales of alcoholic beverages which are to be drastically reduced. If sales of alcoholic beverages were to be included, rates of growth would be lower.[4]

As Table 2 shows, the average annual growth of investment in the machine-building sector is an outstanding figure amounting to no less than 12.5%. This points to the key element of the current Five-Year Plan: "modernization" is to focus on the sector where the bulk of investment goods, consumer durables, and defence material is manufactured. For the time being, priority is apparently to be given to the production of investment goods in order to modernize the equipment within the machine-building sector itself.

Needless to say, the Soviets are not in the business of telling us what is happening to the economic priority of the military. Given the rather high overall growth targets, the plan does not (on paper) impose absolute cuts on consumption, and probably does not imply any absolute cuts for defence. It can, however, be inferred from some statements in speeches by Gorbachev and Ryzhkov that within the engi-

4 Thus, for 1986 the planned figure for retail trade turnover incl. liquor was set at 5.3%, and the realized figure was 6.4%, indicating a higher degree of overfulfillment than the "dry" figures are showing. The figures also show that the anti-alcoholism campaign does not appear to have been as successful as intended. Sources: *Soviet statistical yearbooks*; plan documents; 1986 figures: *Pravda*, 18.01.1987

neering sector which employs about 40 percent of the industrial labour force the share of investment going to civilian industries is to increase from somewhat under half to somewhat over half.

One tentative interpretation of this would be as follows. The defence industry's capacity is for the time being to be increased only moderately. Until the early 1990s the level of output of new military hardware will not increase much. Meanwhile a major effort is going into the development and modernization of a cluster of industries concerned with electronics-based products. That much is evident from the very high targets for the growth of the output of computer equipment (about 18 percent a year between 1985 and 1990). This also means that the high-technology industry which produces components and sub-systems for both military and civilian products would be strengthened, allowing the introduction of more advanced and more competitive weapons systems in the early-to-mid-1990s. Until that time, the capacity for final-stage assembly of military devices could be held roughly constant. That interpretation, to repeat, is tentative and cannot be fully substantiated from material at present in the public domain.

The downgrading of the ceremonial and formal authority of the military leadership under Gorbachev might suggest that this manoeuvre does not have purely military aims, and is perhaps not accepted whole-heartedly by the military. Nor would Gorbachev's calls on military production units to offer more and better civilian side-line production be popular with the military. Such calls, it is true, are only a re-run of sentiments that were expressed by Brezhnev; but it would be characteristic of Gorbachev if they were more energetically followed through.

The changes in priorities have been accompanied by a general tightening of pressure from above on the economic management hierarchy. This has taken the form of generally tauter targets and more activism in penalising failure, corruption and evasion of responsibility. Correspondingly, Gorbachev has imposed a drastic turnover on senior personnel, including the replacement of about 60 out of some 90 ministers and equivalents. That sort of purge could have produced paralysis as everyone became concerned with avoiding trouble and therefore avoiding decisions. In practice the combination of policies seems to have produced an improvement in economic performance from the spring of 1985 through 1986. The relatively poor harvest of 1985 and the severe winter of 1984-5 made the improvement less than obvious at first. So did the statistical fudges connected with the covering up of the effects of the alcohol campaign on Soviet total output as officially measured. (The CIA's measures of GNP do not encounter this problem, so their preliminary estimate of 4.2 percent growth in 1986 was not in conflict with the observations of Western specialists about the Soviet figures for that year being overstated.)

In 1987, however, growth slowed again. In the first three quarters of the year, according to official Soviet data and compared to the corresponding period in 1986, the annual growth rate of national income produced was only 2.4 percent, of industry 3.6, and agriculture 1.1. The reasons for this renewed slowdown are not clear. It is possible that a combination of bad weather and transitional problems (adjustment to organizational change) are to blame, in which case the renewed slowdown would only be temporary. But this is not certain.

3. Reorganization

The so-called reform measures could not have had any impact on performance as yet. But what has been announced is radical by Soviet standards, even though it falls short of a coherent, market-socialist reform plan. In fact, numerous Soviet press reports confirm that even what was announced in 1985-86 has, by and large, not yet been implemented. One would not expect a serious reform to be effective quickly. There is nonetheless a great deal to be said for introducing it as a single package, but Gorbachev's measures have come piecemeal, and are not yet complete.

What is important, therefore, is not what has been announced in decrees up to now, but the general shape and scope of the existing decrees and the further organizational changes that have been foreshadowed. They provide a view of what the "Gorbachev package" contains, and what its effectiveness is likely to be.

Only recently has Gorbachev presided over measures of economic re-organization that could be called radical. In late June, 1987, a package of semi-market-reform measures was adopted by the Party's Central Committee, apparently after the greatest difficulty. It consisted of a new law on the state enterprise, together with a kind of statement of intent about further, complementary changes in the organization and functions of central administrative bodies in the economy. In combination with earlier measures, intended to encourage family enterprises and small cooperatives, and the even more far-reaching draft law on cooperatives published in March 1988 (for detail see below), this batch of laws and decrees aims at a curious kind of halfway-house economic system. What is intended is not a market-socialist reform such as the Hungarians aimed at in 1968 (and have not fully implemented twenty years later). It is nonetheless a significant departure from Soviet practice of the last 55-60 years.

Many elements in the scheme can be traced back to the "optimal planners'" ideas of the early 1960s. These include the naive idea of a harmonious blend of "plan and market". The central planners are supposed to retain control not only over the broad structure of investment and the management of social welfare and defence, but also over a substantial portion of current output and prices. So far as the industrial sector is concerned, this direct micro-economic control is to be exercised chiefly through state orders -- orders in the commercial, not the military sense, but nonetheless obligatory for the enterprise. These will initially cover at least 70 percent of industrial output. For the rest, enterprises are to deal freely with one another, i.e. to operate through the market.

In all sectors, state enterprises are to draft their own annual and five-year plans. These would not require approval by branch ministries. There would in theory be no directive targets "from above" for enterprises. Centralized supply allocation, the cornerstone of the traditional system, is supposed to be replaced largely -- but not entirely -- by "wholesale trade" among producers, distributors and customers. Profits would, in effect, be taxed at rates known in advance, providing enterprises with an incentive to improve quality, expand etc.

However, the control figures and the state orders, plus substantial state price control and centralized allocation of perhaps 300 "key commodities" make the plan/market mixture an awkward one.

The scheme has one saving grace: the encouragement (or rather, attempted encouragement) of legitimate small-scale private and cooperative enterprise in services, agriculture and perhaps some branches of industry. Such units would mostly be outside the planning process and would continue, grow or disappear on their merits in the market. Such small, unplanned units have spread in much of Eastern Europe, and have done a great deal to ease everyday living conditions. In other words, the influence of the center would be concentrated in certain sectors.

There are three main weaknesses, however. First, enterprises will often be receiving signals both from the authorities and from the market, and those signals will often be in conflict with each other. Second, it still is to be expected that branch ministries will act as hierarchical intermediaries between enterprises and the centre; such ministries have powerful reasons to maintain detailed control over "their" enterprises and therefore to circumvent the new rules which forbid them to do more than provide broad guidelines. Third, there is little evidence that market-socialist reforms, let alone semi-market reforms, do anything much for the rate of technological change -- one of Gorbachev's main aims.

By the end of 1987 Gorbachev seemed, for the time being, to have lost a major battle with the economic branch ministries. Earlier he made it fairly clear that he wanted the ministries to be consolidated into a much smaller number of "super-ministries" managing whole "complexes" (fuel and energy, transport, civilian machine-building and other sectors). That proved extremely hard to push through.

If implemented properly so that the number of ministry-level officials were drastically reduced it would have the effect of reducing the ministry's/superministry's capacity to interfere in the detailed operation of the enterprise. (The "enterprise", at least in the producer-goods sector, is also being pushed into amalgamations so that a smaller number of larger units should be the end-result outside the consumer sector.) With the greater authority and freedom from detailed meddling that is supposed to result, the enterprise was to be given more scope for making its own detailed production, and to some extent investment, decisions. In the enterprise law and joint party-state decree on branch ministries of July 17, 1987, however, branch-ministry structure survives intact.

The exact future of the centralized supply system remains unclear. So does the future of price-setting arrangments. Those are crucial elements in any future reform. It is now clear that a serious revision of prices will not occur before 1990. This would be more than just a revision on the lines of earlier attempts. There will this time be some further decentralization of the power to set prices. At present decentralized price-setting powers apply to a very limited range of goods. But enterprises will be given somewhat more scope to set their own prices, within centrally-set guidelines. New industrial wholesale prices will not come in until 1990; new agricultural procurement prices are due in 1991; no date is set for changes in retail prices; and the extent and timing of the devolution of some price-setting powers to enterprises have not been made clear. Finally, the transition to "wholesale trade" in producer goods is yet another important element of the reform whose extent and timing have not been spelt out clearly.

The March 1988 draft law on cooperatives is the most radical piece of economic legislation presented in the Gorbachev era. It goes much further to encourage non-state, and therefore non-planned, economic activity than earlier measures. It contains strong provisions to facilitate private economic initiative. Among other things, cooperatives shall be allowed to act as a legal entity; to have no limits on their size and earnings; to be legally protected by state agencies except for purposes of enforcing the law; to issue shares; and to employ hired (non-member) labour. The justification for describing these provisions as still being "socialist" is that members' incomes will be subject to progressive taxation and that nobody will be permitted to be a non-working member of a producer cooperative -- i.e., to have a purely *rentier* income. To what extent these proposals will be implemented is difficult to say at present. But their potential for changing the economy should not be underestimated.

In sum, the published decrees do not demonstrate a definite commitment by the central authorities to a decisive shift to market relations between enterprises.

There is clearly an *intention* to move in that direction, but an overall market-socialist shape of things to come has not yet been outlined by the authorities.

A partial decentralization of price-setting and the abolition of centralized supply allocation are two crucial elements in a Hungarian-style, market-socialist reform. The implementation of a market-socialist reform, however, should not be regarded as an answer to all the Soviet leadership's primary concerns. Foremost, there is very little reason to think that a market-socialist reform would transform Soviet performance in technological innovation. The limited empirical evidence gives *no encouragment to the view of market socialism as a hospitable environment for rapid technological change*. A priori arguments about the importance of profit and the threat of business failure as spurs to innovation under capitalism suggest the reason for this. Whether it is true or not that socialism and rapid innovation are incompatible, the Soviet leaders are nowhere near putting that proposition to the test, and *glasnost* has not so far extended to the public discussion of any such fundamentally uncomfortable ideas. (Only Larissa Popkova in *Novyi mir*, No. 5, 1987, and Nikolay Shmelev in the following issue have come close to raising this issue.)

In general, the reorganization process so far is a move towards arrangements which are normal in much of Eastern Europe. Patterns for the core of the economy: the producer-goods sector, however, seem to be tailored much more along East German than any other East European lines. Some improvements in growth rates, in product quality and in technological performance may well result from the changes in priorities, pressure and personnel. But it is doubtful whether the resulting amelioration can be sustained in time (beyond, say, five years) and widely diffused across economic branches. It is equally doubtful whether even "Hungarian-style" reforms, which are not at present on the agenda, would in the Soviet Union generate improvements that were both extensive and lasting.

The main qualification to be made to this, from Soviet perspectives, pessimistic prognosis has to do with the very recent moves to expand private and cooperative economic activity. These could significantly improve food and other consumer supplies. If extended to industry and applied more boldly than previous market-type provisions, they could have a more general, positive effect, on the economy.

## 4. Foreign Trade

The reorganization of the Soviet foreign trade system is also, for the most part, of a standard East European type. The authority to negotiate and sign foreign trade contracts has been extended to a number of ministries and production enterprises and is no longer almost totally concentrated in organizations subordinate to the Ministry of Foreign Trade (MFT). In January 1988 the ministry was merged with the body responsible for military and economic aid to form a Ministry of External Economic Relations (MVES). In a strict sense, the MVES is not the top body in the foreign trade system: since 1986 there has been a small "overlord" body for foreign trade as a whole, the State Committee for External Economic Relations (GVK). The real power of the GVK, however, is hard to assess.

Control over the volume and composition of the import bill should not, in principle, be relaxed, though there might be some slippage while the new arrangements are being run in.

Joint ventures with both East European and Western concerns can now be formed on Soviet territory, the Western joint ventures being subject to mandatory Soviet majority shares. "Western" joint venture legislation already exists in all the East European CMEA countries except the GDR, and in several cases has been in place for over a decade without producing dramatic results. The Soviet aims in these organizational changes seem to be chiefly to promote non-fuel exports for hard currency, to get better access to Western technology and mangagement skills and to get greater benefits from CMEA cooperation through reducing bureaucratic impediments to Soviet-East European enterprise contacts.

The limitations of these changes have been widely discussed. It is clear that a satisfactory organizational and legal framework has yet to be created for Western joint ventures. Some joint ventures will no doubt be established, and some of these will probably be assessed as successful by both parties. But East European experience suggests that it will take something like two years, as a rule, to negotiate a joint venture of any consequence and something like five to seven years before it could be said to be running smoothly. At present West European businessmen with substantial commitment to the Soviet market seem on the whole to see a joint venture as something they will have to propose in order to retain good will, but not as something from which they expect very much and therefore not as something in which to invest heavily. Know-how, capitalized at an impressive-looking value, is one form of investment they are likely to employ in order to avoid committing much new capital. The whole joint venture exercise rather resembles the innovation of science-and-technology agreements with Western firms, which was supposed to, but did not, have a great influence on East-West trade and Soviet economic performance in the 1970s. Nonetheless, in 1987 over 20 "Western" joint ventures in the USSR were signed. They are generally on a small scale, but spread across a wide range of activities.

More important for Soviet-Western trade prospects than such schemes is the development of the Soviet domestic economy and of its capacity to produce internationally competitive manufactures. Equally important is the future course of world energy prices. If the oil price remained around or just under $20 a barrel, Soviet hard-currency energy export earnings in the developed West in 1990 could be back approximately to the level of 1984 (around $19 billion). Energy sales accounted for four-fifth of hard currency earned in the West (the total excludes arms and other sales to LDCs (Less Develop Countries) and also does not take into account revenue from gold, and services such as shipping). In the medium term, in other words, an approximate stagnation of Soviet hard-currency import capability is a reasonable projection unless the leadership is prepared to sanction a sustained increase in debt-export ratios -- for which there is some scope as far as Western banks are concerned. Further improvement of political relations between Moscow and Washington following the Washington arms control agreement could encourage the Soviets to borrow more and allow US banks to participate directly and openly in such lending. Whether Soviet financial-political caution would be relaxed somewhat under those circumstances so as to allow a substantial growth of such borrowing, is much less clear.

The present Soviet strategy seems to rely more heavily than before on cooperation within CMEA (Council of Mutual Economic Aid), and to keep "dependence" on Western technology modest. In the mid-1980s the Soviet planners seem to have regarded machinery imports from the West as equivalent to about one-tenth of their annual investment in new machinery, and imports from Eastern Europe as equivalent of about one-fifth. The volume of machinery imports from Eastern Europe had been rising faster than that from the West in 1981-85, according to calculations by the United Nations European Economic Commission (8.4 percent a year, against 5.9), and it appears to be Soviet policy to continue along those lines. However, East European capacity to deliver a sharply increased volume in 1986-90 is much reduced because of the very low level of investment in Eastern Europe since the late 1970s. And that is quite apart from the quality issue. Furthermore, Soviet ruble earnings in Eastern Europe should decline due to the delayed effect of the 1985-86 fall in oil prices, since energy looms large in Soviet exports to CMEA as well as to Western countries. The reduction of the big accumulated East European debt to the USSR in the next few years (from which Poland is spared until 1989) goes some way to offset this effect, but in general the Soviet ruble capacity to import from Eastern Europe will not be buoyant. The pressures leading the USSR back to more intensive development of trade with the West seem to be quite strong, but so are the impediments.

## 5. Conclusions and Prospects

According to this analysis the Gorbachev leadership will probably achieve some improvement in general economic performance over perhaps a five-year period.

This view is based on the premise that the changes in priorities, pressure and personnel can have more than short run (say, up to two years) effect. Gorbachev is presiding over a switch of resources into research and development plus engineering production, and these are the sectors which generate most new technology embodied in new machinery. One does not expect the pay-off to those additional resources to be as high as it would be under competitive capitalism, but it should at least be positive. If the resource shift occurred mainly at the expense of projects of the kind exemplified by the BAM railway and the Siberian river-diversion scheme, it could even be fairly painless. Similarly, increased pressure and personnel changes may well be capable of generating more output from given inputs without changes in the system simply by reducing organizational slack. The amount of slack (relative to potential output) by the end of the Brezhnev era was by general consent large, and there is no strong reason to assume that its reduction is a process that must occur within a short space of time.

The priorities which Gorbachev favours centre on engineering output and equipment investment. Both of these activities are particularly vulnerable, within the Soviet system, to hidden inflation through the use of phoney product innovation by enterprise managers and ministry officials to gain *de facto* price increases which are not captured in the official price indices. There is likely therefore to be an element of apparent improvements in officially-reported performance that will be attributable to a statistical illusion. In other words, Gorbachev's priorities happen to be the ones which the Soviet system is particularly good at pretending to meet. But still there can also be some genuine improvement. The better performance of the previously-troubled oil, coal and steel industries since early 1985 exemplifies this sort of real change.

The Soviet reform process might over time become more radical. It might even prove possible to invigorate Soviet performance in innovation while retaining predominantly socialist ownership and the party's monopoly of political power. The relevant point is that *"reforms" are unlikely to have much impact on Soviet economic performance in the foreseeable future (up to 1990)*, except insofar as the encouragement of small-scale private and cooperative ventures outside the planning system produces some improvement in everyday life for Soviet citizens -- a development which would be of no direct and very little indirect consequence for Soviet foreign policy. The other intended changes are not meant to be operational before 1991.

The best objective test of the success of Gorbachev's economic strategy will be the Soviet share in Western imports of manufactures, which at present is tiny and has tended to decline since the mid-1960s. (A rise in protectionism would complicate this assessment.) Another test would be the degree of satisfaction on the part of Soviet military planners with the military technology available to them in the mid-1990s. That test, however, will be even harder for outsiders to apply.

What matters most for the outside world in the short run is the bearing Gorbachev's economic policies will have on the Soviet military effort and on trade. In the longer run it is the success of his policies as a whole. Certainly, a lasting revitalization of the Soviet economy would be good for Soviet domestic political stability. It would help improve Soviet international prestige and the USSR's capacity to attract foreign admiration and support. For example, CMEA cooperation would be more attractive for Eastern Europe; the Soviet model would look more convincing economically in the Third World; and the West European left, the peace movement and some groups in the West European social mainstream would also be more favourably inclined towards Moscow. But it could also mean, finally, that Soviet military potential would be bigger than it would otherwise be.

Such a strengthening of the "Soviet challenge" in the longer run is more likely to be achieved by a strategy which includes a short-run relative *decline in the priority given to the military*: not necessarily an absolute cut in the military effort, but a period in which the resource allocations to the military are somewhat less than they would have been on unchanged policies. There is no way of proving that Gorbachev and his closest associates share this view, but there are some signs that they do. It is in that sense that Gorbachev is seeking some kind of *peredyshka* (breathing space). To suggest this is not necessarily to take a cynical view of Soviet intentions. It does not follow that Soviet readiness to make concessions in arms control talks must be a clever manoeuvre simply aimed at lulling the Western alliance into a false sense of security in order the better to seize a military advantage at some future date. Either a permanent or a temporary reduction in tension might be welcome to the Kremlin. For the time being, the Soviet leaders do not have to choose between them. And they have to be prepared for competition in military technology to continue to be severe, whatever they would prefer.

## *III. The Defence Economy: Burden or Asset?*

### 1. Levels, Trends and Variations in Military Outlays

It is still too early to assess a "trend" of defence spending after Gorbachev's access to power. There has been some dispute between the Central Intelligence

Agency (CIA) and the Defence Intelligence Agency (DIA ) as to whether and how much Soviet military expenditures have increased in 1983 and 1984, and whether one could speak of a new upward trend after 1982. The dispute has made it clear that intelligence estimates have to be used very cautiously with respect to the most recent years. As the CIA has pointed out on several occasions, its estimates are too rough for exactly assessing year-by-year changes. As a result, the agency has always preferred to present long-term average growth rates. Bearing in mind this reservation, its current assessments -- shared by British and West German estimates -- are that no significant change has occurred yet in Soviet military expenditure under Gorbachev.

According to British estimates Soviet military spending has risen in constant (1982) prices from around 75 billion rubles in 1970 to around 110 billion rubles in 1986 (in current prices from 50 billion to 130 billion rubles). Such estimates by far exceed the amount officially released by the Soviet Union in its annual defence budget. The sum total published now stands at 20 billion rubles. However, deputy foreign minister Vladimir Petrovsky recently revealed that the published total constituted only a part of total expenditure. All procurement and research, development and testing, he said, were not included in the figures.

As for long-term trends in military spending, the two US intelligence agencies concur that the average annual growth rate has become markedly lower since the mid-1970s (2 percent in constant prices) as compared to the preceding decade (4-5 percent). Measured in current prices, the share of defence expenditure in the Soviet GNP (by Western definition) has continued to increase, from an already high number of 12-14 percent in the early 1970s to about 15-17 percent at present. This is almost three times the corresponding share in the United States. Both the size of, and the increase in, the Soviet defence burden seem to suggest that the long-term policy to let military outlays grow faster than GNP cannot be maintained any longer.

Yet it is doubtful whether the traditional policy could not be continued for quite some time -- even though at a certain "growth-price" for the economy. In order to examine the possible effects of high or low growth of, and cuts in, military spending it is instructive to apply a simple econometric model.[5] However simple the model may be it does consider:

5 Details of the model stucture are reported in Franz Walter, *"What Increase in GNP Can the Soviets Expect by Lowering the Growth of Military Outlays?"*, in: Murry Feshbach, *National Security Issues of the USSR*, Proceedings of a NATO Colloquium, November 5-8, 1986 (Dordrecht: Martinus Nijhoff, 1987), pp. 200-229.

:isely, of Net Material Product -- NMP) as a
ıl, in the labour force, and in overall productiv-
, the latter representing "technological pro-
st meaning.

n investment funds of preceding years; such
after subtraction of consumption and defence

/th rate for consumption (say 2 percent p.a.),
with alternative rates of increase or decrease
ıre, it is assumed that any variation in defence
ı unrealistic assumption yet intended not to
of, NMP growth.

in Chart 1. The vertical axis in the chart
P, each curve being attributed to a certain
1984, when the growth rate of NMP was 3.3

As can be seen, there is a marked asymmetry between the cases of decreasing and of increasing defence spending. When spending is to increase by 2.4 or more percent, the NMP growth rates will continously decline throughout the period of consideration. When spending is to decrease, NMP growth will accelerate (if only modestly) for just some years, say up to 1990, and will slow down somewhat thereafter. Even with a reduction of the military expenditure by 10 percent in every year during the 1985-1995 period, by which its share in NMP would be diminished to a value of as low as 6.4 percent in 1990 and to even 3.2 percent in 1995, NMP growth would be enhanced by no more than half a percentage point. On the other hand, speeding up military expenditures by 10 percent (almost one third of national income would then be spent on defence in 1995!) would significantly reduce NMP growth (to 1.8 percent).

One may wonder whether in case of a perceived marked increase in the threat, a slow-down of NMP growth to 2 percent and below might not be felt still to be acceptable. In these conditions it would seem that an average rate of growth of defence expenditures of up to 5 percent p.a., or even somewhat more, would still be manageable in the medium term. This would correspond with the historical rate of increase (in current prices). However, in this case no acceleration of economic growth would be possible, not to speak of attaining the NMP growth rate of 4.2 percent as stipulated by the Five-Year Plan.

*Chart 1 - Development of the NMP Growth Rate due to Variations in the Growth Rate of Defence Spending*

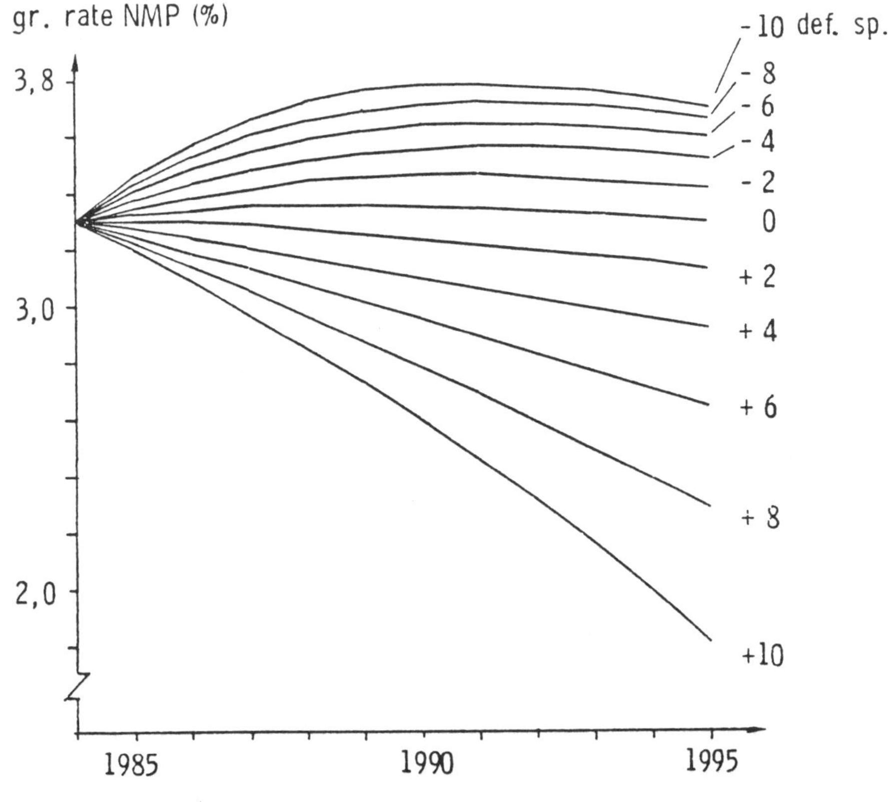

The curious asymmetry of the model outcome can easily be explained: when defence spending grows by a constant rate, it will develop in an exponential fashion, subtracting more and more from investment funds every year. When, on the other hand, defence spending is reduced by a constant rate, it will develop in a logarithmic fashion, adding less and less to investment funds.

The generally limited impact of defence variations on NMP growth is due to two factors: (1) Any realistic variation in the defence budget is small in comparison with the volume of existing investment funds. (2) Any variation in investment is also small in comparison with the volume of capital stocks; just the growth of the latter bears on the growth of NMP.

There is therefore only, it appears, a limited incentive for the Soviet government to reduce defence spending so as to enhance economic growth; there are comparatively strong reasons for avoiding a rapid increase in the allocation of resources for military purposes.

Economic performance, as both the model and common sense suggest, can only be improved by far-reaching reform measures. Combined with such measures, deep cuts in military expenditures would contribute to overcome the "war economy"-character of the present system, leaving more room for satisfying the needs of the consumer. The effects on growth of such a transformation of the Soviet economic system cannot be assessed by the model; its parameters reflect the present economic mechanism.

Short off an acceleration of overall economic growth, the Soviet leadership, by cutting defence spending, may have in mind more specific yet nevertheless important effects such as improvements in certain key sectors of the economy. As already demonstrated, "modernization" throughout the economy, but particularly in the machine-building sector, is a major objective of the Gorbachev leadership. Hence, if scarce high-quality materials and high technology components (e.g electronics) were used to a lesser extent for the production of weaponry and made available for the production of investment goods, modernization of important economic sectors could undoubtedly be promoted.

Similarly, the defence industry which has for a long time been engaged in the production of a whole range of civilian goods might have to expand this very role. In fact, such expansion appears to be the easiest and most effective method to achieve a certain transfer of productive capacity from the military to the civilian sector.

2. Cuts and Consequences

But what about the prospects and problems of specific cuts? Three different areas can be distinguished where the "axe" could fall: the stretching of procurement, and research and development programmes; manpower reductions; and curtailment of operations, maintenance, exercises and training. In all of these areas, disctinctions have to be made as to short-term and long-term effects.

As for procurement costs, cuts in nuclear forces are unlikely to produce direct financial benefit let alone significant reductions in the level of defence spending. Decommissioning costs for strategic systems are heavy and would offset the financial gains of operating and maintaining a smaller force. Verification, where it includes on-site inspection (as, for instance, in the December 1987 Washington agreement on intermediate-range nuclear forces), could also prove expensive. But even in the long term the savings would be modest. This is due to the comparatively small share of nuclear forces in overall military expenditure and to the requirement of modernization of the remaining force.

Major savings can only be made in the conventional field. This is because of the concentration of expenditure (approximately 80 percent) on general purpose forces. Furthermore, considerable scope exists for savings given the significant Warsaw Pact superiority over NATO in weapons stocks of many types and the long-standing Soviet inclination to pursue simultaneously, on a belt and braces principle, more than one programme for a single, or for closely related, purposes.

But majors savings will most likely materialize only in the long run. In the short term one might even expect overall military expenditure to rise in real terms by some 2,5 percent over 1987-1992. This projection would be based on the fact that for most weapons systems the period from conception to obsolescence lasts many years, and that almost all major weapons for which procurement and operational expenditure are likely to be incurred through the early 1990's are already known (as are a large proportion of those on which research and development outlays may be made). This remaining projection, however, presupposes that established patterns are not altered by policy changes. And indeed, perhaps with the exception of naval shipbuilding, there is so far no evidence that equipment plans are being reviewed on financial or other grounds.

But even with a change of course and the cancellation or reduction of weapons programmes in scope and time, costs in terms of wasted resources still tend to be considerable once decisions have been taken to move from the research stage to development, and heavy outlays have been incurred for such things as buildings, manufacturing equipment and prototypes. Moreover, in the Soviet Union the latter outlays may be relatively greater than in the West owing to the practice of constructing additional facilities for new programmes rather then merely refitting the older ones. For these reasons and because of the long lead times in fielding new equipment, cutbacks now would not yield substantial savings until the 1990's.

As for cuts in the size of the Soviet armed forces the cost/benefit analysis must be equally complex. On the one hand, the potential savings on personnel costs are relatively small given existing pay levels of a largely conscripted force and continued ideological commitment to the value of mass conscription. Personnel costs currently account for only about 8 percent of the total budget. There is considerable benefit to the economy from the training given to conscripts as, for instance, familiarity with certain technological and managemen skills which are of use when conscripts are released back into the labour force.

On the other hand release of manpower to the economy could be of some importance. This is true despite Gorbachev's (and his predecessors'!) emphasis on "intensive" economic growth, i.e. increasing the productivity of labour and manpower rather than on extensive development or increasing the volume of inputs. Intensive and extensive growth, however, are complements, not substitutes. At present the labour force is down to a growth rate of about 0.4 percent a year; there is substantial undermanning of existing industrial capacity; and investment growth is being stepped up. Any sizeable addition to the civilian labour force should, in those circumstances, be welcome to Soviet policy makers.

All remaining possibilities would yield only marginal savings. Most of the expenditure on operations and maintenance goes on spare parts and servicing, and cutbacks on a major scale would prove counterproductive. Economizing on fuel could provide some savings but the penalties in reduced training and hence readiness would be large. There is little evidence of fuel preservation by the ground or air forces. But there is evidence for cuts in Soviet naval exercises around the world.

### 3. The Military's Attitude Towards Economic Affairs

Whether the Soviet military supports Gorbachev's economic and arms control policy is an important problem that needs to be carefully considered. This is true even if the military's political influence has further declined under his rule, as some Western observers believe. Clearly, the professional military officers' expertise is needed -- and very successfully used in arms control negotiations. And if it is true, as most Western Kremlinologists assume, that Gorbachev's policies are controversial and that opposition to them exists, and that even the ouster of the General Secretary (or something even worse) cannot at all be excluded from the realm of possibilities, it does matter on whose side the leaders of the armed forces ultimately decide to stand.

An authoritative work edited by Marshal Akhromeyev in 1986 says: "In the history of war, there are known several cases where the great possibilities of the state have not been used, and the army has suffered defeat. An enormous advantage of the USSR and the other socialist states consists of the fact that socialism and the leadership of the Marxist-Leninist party assures, in case of war, the more accelerated, the more comprehensive, and the more effective use of all resources and possibilities of the state for the achievement of victory over the aggressor."[6]

To be sure, quite the same was said in the 1983 edition of this work as in other previous military writings. But this is precisely the point: basic attitudes of the Soviet military towards defence economics are being expressed here, and it appears that the generals have not changed their minds during the first two years of Gorbachev's rule. Their message is clear:

- The socialist (read: centralized) economic system allows for the full mobilization of resources for military purposes in case of war but also in peace-time. The armed forces have always, because of the possibility of a sudden surprise attack, to be prepared immediately to rebuff an aggression. They have to maintain combat readiness on a high level. And they must be equipped with the newest weaponry. The initial period of an eventual future war will be decisive, so peace-time preparation is of overriding importance.
- What in Western or in some Soviet civilian eyes may appear as a heavy burden on the economy also has major advantages, the military claims. There is spill-over from the military to the civilian sector, and even now more than 40 per cent of the total output of the military-industrial plants is for civilian usage.
- When doing less than what can be done for strengthening defence, defeat will be the consequence in a possible war, the military warns.

Hence, the Soviet military will certainly plead not to change the basic elements of the present centralized "war-economy" system, and it will of course argue against attributing a negative value to defence efforts in principle.

However, this basic position does not rule out the possibility that the military leadership agrees with modest growth of defence spending, or no growth at all, during certain periods. Such a period may apply at present. Western experts by and

---

6 S. Akromyeyev et al. (ed.), *Voyennyi entsikopedicheskii slovar'*, 2nd edition (Moscow: Voyenizdat, 1986), p. 151.

large agree that a decisive factor for the continuing slow increase in Soviet defence spending since the mid-1970s has been the deceleration of economic growth. If the Soviet military shares this opinion, they themselves must have become interested in an improvement of the economic situation.

Military concern about the USSR's economic position has been expressed, for instance, by one of the Deputies to the Chief of the General Staff, Garyeyev, in 1985. "Weaponry", he wrote, "becomes more and more expensive, and we are confronted with adversaries being considerably stronger in economic terms than ever before. Therefore, military-theoretical thinking has constantly to elaborate on methods as to how to make use most effectively of the means which, within the limits of strict necessity, are provided for military needs, so that our defence is reliable, and, at the same time, is not too great a burden for the state."[7]

Soviet officers are probably most concerned about the USSR's state of the art in science and technology. Throughout the seventies, heavy investments were undertaken in military research and development in order to reduce or even close the technology gap *vis-à-vis* the West. However, the production of the highly sophisticated new weapons seems to have met some difficulties in the defence industry, which in turn has been regarded by Western observers as another factor for the slow-down of the growth of military expenditures. The arms production sector may have found it increasingly difficult to receive high quality input materials from civilian industry and consequently may have experienced its own problems with manufacturing. If so, the military leadership may not fail to resist but may even *support* the modernization program for the machine-building sector.

The military will consider *modernizatsiya* all the more urgent, since -- as Marshal Ogarkov has written in a well-known treatise in 1985 -- "a revolutionary change in military affairs is going on in our times."[8] This change, he argues, is connected with the further improvement in nuclear weaponry but also, and even more so, with an enormous sophistication of conventional systems. In the West, Soviet military writers are warning, great efforts are being made to integrate modern means of reconnaissance, and command and control, with attack aircraft and medium-range missiles into coherent detect-and-strike complexes *(razvedyvatel'no-udarnye kompleksy)* designed to destroy advancing tank formations or the Warsaw Pact's air defence system, and that this were connected with Western war-fighting concepts of "forward defence" and "deep strike" operations. In this context SDI, too, is perceived as an important project that would speed up the military-technological competition.

7 M.A. Garyeyev, *M.V. Frunze--voyennyi teoretik* (Moscow: Voyenizdat, 1985), p.425.
8 Marshal N.V. Ogarkov, *Istoriya uchit bditel'nosti* (Moscow: Voyenizdat, 1985), p. 41.

Clearly, from the Soviet military's perspective the "revolution in military-technological affairs" at present rests heavily upon electronics. And in this respect it seems that things have been reversed in the last three decades: Whereas in the 1960s and early 1970s the spillover of military research and development into civilian branches of industry was considered an important subject, the *dependence of defence technology on the overall scientific and technological progress*, primarily in the field of data processing and transmission, has now become the relevant issue for discussion. The Soviet military seems to be aware of this and also of the fact that the West is leading in this critical area of science.

Distinctly unpleasant to the military establishment, however, is probably the fact that Gorbachev is determined to apply *perestroika* to the military realm. This became evident in several articles starting from the beginning of 1987, including by the previous defence minister, Marshal Sokolov, in March. But the calls for major changes in military affairs have become more insistent after the "Rust affair" (the landing of the West German student in Moscow's Red Square at the end of May 1987) under the new defence minister, General Dmitri Yazov. Such calls can, of course, mean many things. But foremost they aim at greater discipline, better training, more dedication and participation, and greater efficiency in meeting defence requirements within the present budget, i.e. doing more with less. Since such aims are consistent with the military's value system there is very little they can do but to support them.

## 4. Conclusions and Prospects

To sum up, the military's support for *perestroika* and Gorbachev's policy of modernizing the economy and accelerating production is only partial. They most likely regard the current state of civil-military relations as some kind of a standstill agreement.[9] After some years they would probably want to see the reward for their patience in terms of not only *more* but of *better* equipment for the armed forces.

As for the larger issues it would be erronous to assume that Gorbachev is being compelled by economic constraints to conclude arms control agreements with the West. He may very well be aware of the fact that in the short term neither political decisions nor the successful conclusion of arms control agreements will have a significant impact on the level of defence expenditure.

As for the long term, economic performance can only be improved by "intensification" and "modernization", which in turn crucially depends on structural reforms

9 For a more detailed discussion of civil-military relations see below, ch. IV, sect. 4.

and on changes in attitudes and behavior of the managers, workers, and government and party officials.

But the effects of major structural changes can be enhanced by economizing in the military sector, and by a shift of resources and personnel from the military to the civilian sector (or perhaps more appropriately, to certain key sectors of the civilian economy). Conversely, given the asymmetrical effects of increased, as against decreased, military spending on economic performance), Gorbachev has good reason to be worried about a sharpening of the military-technological competition and an increase in pressures on the long-run growth of civilian output. This does provide incentives for reducing competitive pressures with the West.[10]

## *IV. Domestic Political Change: "Restructuring", "Openness", "Democratization" -- The Demise of "Stalinism"*

### 1. What Is New Since 1985?

What has changed in the Soviet domestic politics since Gorbachev's ascendancy to power in March 1985? One problem is that Gorbachev the reformer has come to the open only in 1987. After a relatively uneventful start in 1985 the new party leader had a difficult time in the first half of 1986 during which he displayed great caution. Thus, the 27th party congress still remained very much under the influence of "acceleration" (*uskorenie*). But as the year progressed, "democratization" and "*glasnost*" came to be stressed more and more. The realization took stronger hold, and was expressed more clearly, that modernization of the economy was impossible without far-raching change in ideology, society, and politics. A "big leap forward" in reformist effort took place in the fall of 1986 and early 1987, above all to be observed at the January and June 1987 plenary meetings of the Communication Center (CC). Starting from the summer this was followed by a reassertion of "socialist conservative" tendencies culminating in November 1987 in the dramatic dismissal of the reformist Moscow city party chief and candidate member of the Politburo, Bosis Yeltsin. Even though conservative critics, including in the Politburo, are still carefully watching, the political position of the General Secretary has improved. The escalation of slogans, from "acceleration" in 1985 to "restructuring", "radical reform" and "revolution" in 1986 and 1987, together with the deepening and widening policy of "openness", illustrate the evolution of Gorbachev's reformist policies.

10 For more detail concerning interrelationships between these issues and Soviet foreign policy see below, ch. V, sect. 5.

It is, of course, not the first time that a leader in Moscow has tried to improve and modernize the Soviet system. Parallels and similarities with Khrushchev's reformist efforts in the 1950s and the 1960s are evident. But there are also important differences.

First, *the context has changed*. When Stalin died in 1953, the Soviet economy had not exhausted its capacity to ensure "extensive" growth by the extraction of ever more raw materials and the migration of ever more peasants to the cities. Today the Soviet leaders are faced with a scarcity of raw materials and labour resources. But the newest factor is that economic stagnation has brought about a general deterioration of the social climate: a doubling in twenty years of alcohol consumption; increase in corruption; the growth of illegal black maket activities; deepening of disillusionment, even despair, among the new generation and the cultural elite; and the spreading of irresponsibility and indiscipline, as illustrated in the past two years by the Chernobyl catastrophe, the Admiral Nakhimov and other human and ecological disasters, as well as by the "Rust affair" which showed that this situation had also spread to the military. All of this was known by observers abroad but attempts were made by Brezhnev to cover it up. Today this situation is clearly admitted and exploited by Gorbachev's supporters to explain the urgent need for change. Their strength derives from the fact that the opponents of reform have no alternative to propose. The latters' only argument is that the conditions are not as bad as portrayed by Gorbachev. But this is not a program.

Second, the original feature of the Gorbachevian approach is the assumption that any economic progress cannot be brought about by mere bureaucratic reorganization of the management system, as it was envisaged in the past (and notably under Khrushchev), but that reorganization needed to be supplemented by *democratization of the Soviet society across the board, including a democratization of the political system*. This was clearly and credibly stated by Georgi Shakhnazarov, first deputy head of the CC department for relations with the socialist countries, president of the Soviet Political Science Association and one of Gorbachev's many advisors, when he explained to an American journalist in April 1987 that the policy of openness and the proposed election reforms had essentially developed by improvisation. "The first idea was to use old methods to speed scientific and technical development. Shortly they realized that this was impossible without the full participation of the entire society."[11]

In that respect "de-Stalinization", which has come again to be the order of the day, may be less colourful, emotional and dramatic than its counterpart under Khrushchev but it is also broader and deeper. In its current form it involves a

11 Don Oberndorfer, *Washington Post*, 26 April 1987, pp. D1/D4.

denunciation not only of the Great Terror, but also of the collectivization, a rehabilitation of Bukharin (the man and his doctrine), Trostky (the man at least), and new approaches to history, sociology and culture.

At the same time, may be because he is not yet able or willing to impose the necessary institutional changes, the new party leader continues to emphasize the traditional methods of propaganda, exhortation, and agitprop. *Perestroika* is thus up to now much more a matter of pressure and change of personnel inside the same system, rather than a programme of institutional change.[12] This is a weakness in Gorbachev's current design.

Third, while everything which is said today about financial autonomy (*khozraschet*), direct links between companies, even market, is not quite new: it was already largely discussed in earlier periods, including under Stalin as far as *khozrastchet* is concerned. What is really new is the emphasis put by Gorbachev, especially after the June Plenum in 1987, *on the private sector, its potential role in agriculture as well as in the development of services and light industry*. Here Gorbachev and his ally Yakovlev go further than any of their predecessors since the promulgation of the New Economic Policy (NEP) by Lenin in 1921. But this emphasis has to be translated into realities, which is still far from evident at this point.

Fourth, in the political arena, one important achievement of the new leadership has been *a reshuffle and renewal of cadres at all levels*. This was expected, after two decades of stagnation and "petrification" under Brezhnev. A comparison with two succession periods of the past (after Stalin's death and Khrushchev's ouster, see Annex, Tables I and II) shows that the renewal rate under Gorbachev has been higher than in the previous two cases. But this assessment has to be qualified somewhat:

- Exept for minor adjustments in the governmental apparatus the reshuffle has not been accompanied by any real institutional change. Hence, for example, the composition of the Central Committee, in terms of its functions and the distribution of its membership between party and government officials, the military, and representatives from other institutions, is nearly exactly the same in 1986 as in 1981 (Annex, Table III). Turnover of personnel has been more rapid than before, but constituencies and their respective weight have remained the same.

---

12 For details concerning pressures, and changes in personnel and priorities, in the economic sphere see above, ch. II, sect. 2.

This could change if Gorbachev were to change more thoroughly the political functioning of the system or the way the leaders are appointed. His idea (aired at the January 1987 plenum, not approved by the CC, but applied since then in some places) of having competitive yet still non-secret elections of the party secretaries at various levels might have this result. But there is no trend towards a diminution of the party rule and prerogatives.

- The rejuvenation of cadres has been less pronounced than is generally believed. A comparison of the appointments in the first two years of Brezhnev and of Gorbachev (Annex, Table VII) shows that the new cadres of the former were younger than those of today. In the CC itself, the septuagenarians are a strong minority (10 percent). The renewal rate there has been equal to that of the 20th Congress of 1956 (40 percent), but less than in 1961 (62,8 percent), 1952 and, of course, 1939 after the Great Purge (Annex, Table IV). In the Politburo, Gorbachev is the third most senior member (after Shcherbitsky and Gromyko) in terms of tenure, but still the youngest. The paradox is easily explainable: one consequence of the stagnation of top cadres under Brezhnev has been an excessive aging of the middle level, where replacements have to be found.
- The stagnation rate, i.e. the percentage of leaders having the same position today as at the end of Brezhnev's rule five years ago is higher in the provinces than in the center (Annex, Tables V and VI). The main exeption to the rule is Central Asia, where devastating purges have occurred. By contrast, the leaderhips in the Ukraine, the Baltic states and Azerbaidzhan have been remarkably stable. Nevertheless, this has begun to change in the last few months.

Fifth, the *influence, impact, and visibility of academic specialists with training in complex analysis has increased.* There has been a certain shift towards problem-solvers and away from ideologists. Gorbachev's speeches demonstrate a familiarity with the vocabulary and concepts of modern sociology and political science. He freely and frequently uses such terms as "political culture", "social groups", "feedback", and "corrective mechanisms". The influence of scientists and intellectuals of high calibre, whom he is known to consult, and of his sociologist wife, is probably making itself felt. Gorbachev is the first Soviet leader since Lenin who has what can genuinely be called a higher education; like Lenin he was trained as a lawyer and knows foreign languages. The result is a more realistic, sophisticated and pragmatic form of leadership centred around Gorbachev and a close circle of advisors.

Sixth, the new *party leader has extended the scope of human rights* in the Soviet Union. He has allowed Andrei Sakharov to leave exile, granted pardon to well-known dissidents, and allowed many of them to emigrate and some of them to return. The practice of locking up politically "deviant" but medically entirely sane people in psychiatric hospitals is being openly criticized; new laws to prevent abuse are under preparation. Other legal reforms are to provide the citizen with more rights against arbitrary adminstrative acts. Obviously, such measures have a two-fold rationale. On the one hand they are to increase the backing among the population, foremost among the *intelligentsia* for his policies; on the other they are to enhance the Soviet Union's image in world politics and help recoup some of the lost power of attraction which the Soviet model still possessed in the 1950s.

Seventh, in the cultural area the *most striking aspect of Gorbachevism is "glasnost", or the policy of "openness"*. In fact, and short of a real breakthrough in the institutional or economic areas, this is the main achievement of the new leadership until now. In practice, *glasnost* means several different things:

- The opening of new areas of information and comment. Since Chernobyl, taboos have been lifted on the coverage by Soviet media of natural and human catastrophes, social phenomena like illness, crime, divorce, abortion, and drug addiction, with a corresponding declassification of some statistics. This has a political significance in the Soviet Union, where the Party is traditionally supposed to be responsible for everything and prefers to handle as "non-events" what happens outside its control. At the same time, a new interest for the "human factor" has brought about a wave of opinion polls. This also means a departure from traditional dogmas according to which the Soviet population is "monolithic" and fully supporting the party. The latter could now abandon the myth of "99 percent" yes-votes in elections. But this did not yet happen in the 1987 local elections.

- In terms of content, *glasnost* means a freer tone to address social issues, an extension of the scope of targets open to criticism, including the military. More significantly, it has opened the way to a new appraisal of history -- always a sensitive subject in the USSR -- with a renewed wave of de-Stalinization, a (veiled) criticism of collectivization, a new, more positive, judgement on Khrushchev and a rather radical criticism of stagnation under Brezhnev. A number of previously banned writers have been rehabilitated, and their works have been published.

Openness has created considerable interest in the West, in the Soviet Union (were the overall circulation of newspapers has increased by 15 million copies), and in Eastern Europe (where *Pravda* and other newspapers now, for the first time, find a genuine readership). But it is essential also to note the limits of *glasnost*:

- The lifting of taboos has left untouched large areas of public life, still covered by secrecy. This concerns, first, *the military sector.* With the exception of minor cracks in the wall of secrecy (e.g. the visit by Westerners to the phased array radar station at Krasnoyarsk in Siberia and the chemical weapons factory at Zhikhany at the Volga river, as well as the consent to on-site-inspection in the context of arms control agreements)[13] the most important aspects of military affairs remain concealed. This concerns the size and composition of the military budget, the strength, organization, and deployment of the Soviet armed forces, the priorities in military research and development, the scope and rates of weapons production, and the volume, composition and geographical and distribution of arms exports and military assistance. Second, the KGB is largely exempted from criticism. Third, as for Soviet *foreign policy*, all new initiatives are still being announced after they have been decided. Fourth, the *decision making* process at large, including the discussions in the Politburo and other internal debates as, for instance, at the Central Committe plenums, remain unpublished. Hence, in order to gain insights traditional methods of "Kremlinology" remain necessary.

- *Glasnost* is mainly used by some national, Moscow-based news media; it has not had a big effect, despite the regrets and appeals of Gorbachev, in the provinces. In Moscow itself, even though *Pravda*, *Izvestiya*, television and some other big media play their part in *glasnost*, the main mouthpieces of the campaign are such media as have up to now only had a limited circulation or were nearly unknown, like *Moscow News* (now with a circulation of over one million copies, one quarter of it in Russian), *Ogonyok* and a few others.

- There have neither been major institutional changes in the management of the media and culture, nor in the way in which editors are appointed and decisions made. With one exeption (the unofficial and so far unauthorized *Glasnost* magazine), the whole area remains under the control of the party secretariat and its propaganda department, with its dual subordination to leaders with different points of view: Yegor Ligachev and Alexandr Yakovlev. For this reason, this part of the reform still seems reversible, with the possibility of new instructions imposing a return to orthodoxy. This happened at various moments in Soviet history (and is now happening in China). This explains the "wait-and-see" attitude of many reform-minded writers or journalists, and the

---

13 Such cracks in the wall of military secrecy are discussed further in ch. V, sect. 5.

pressure exerted privately on the most active spokesmen of the policy of openness.

Whereas *glasnost* is the main new aspect of Gorbachev's policies, it is by the same token the one where there is the most outspoken resistance and opposition. What, then, is the position of Gorbachev, his power and authority in the Party, and the future of his leadership?

## 2. Gorbachev's Power and Authority

Two different problems have to be considered:

First, the *Central Committee* of the party with its 306 full members is still not the decision making body which Gorbachev would like it to be. It remains the most important concentration of the high-ranking *nomenklatura*, a place where dissident voices can be heard and objections raised. In this respect its present composition cannot satisfy Gorbachev. More than half of the full members have carried over from the Brezhnev period and of the 1981 Congress, more than a third were there ten years ago, and one tenth are septuagenarians of the "Stalin generation" (see Annex, Table III). Among the last category, some oldtimers clearly identified with conservatism and stagnation were surprisingly reelected in March 1986, although they had been pensioned off in 1985. These included Tikhonov, Brezhnev's head of government; Ponomarev, the veteran kominternist who for 30 years ruled the International Department of the CC; even Baybakov, a symbol of the administrative way of management who chaired the Gosplan almost since Stalin's time; and some old military leaders like Gorshkov and Tolubko. Their reelection to the CC, while important Gorbachev's supporters like Aganbegyan were left out, was a clear sign that the old generation wanted to be there and listened to.

This situation explains why Gorbachev has demanded that a party conference be convened earlier than the regular party congress in 1991. This has been accepted for June 1988, but a struggle has already started to decide whether that conference will be entitled to elect a new Central Committee, as the General Secretary wants, or to make only minor changes in this body, as some opponents say, who are supported by past experience (notably the last party conference, held in 1941). The way in which the issue will be resolved will be an important indicator of Gorbachev's strength.

Second, the *Politburo* remains the main political decision making body, as well as the only place of true debate. Its composition has significantly changed in the past three years: From the ten full members present at Chernenko's death, five have been excluded, the remaining five have been joined by eight new leaders who are now a majority of the 13 members. In the secretariat, out of nine members in March 1985, six have left and ten arrived. More importantly, eight of the present thirteen secretaties have been elected in a very short period, i.e. only since the last party congress in 1986.

But this does not mean that all new members of the leadership are enthusiastic Gorbachev's supporters. The Politburo most likely contains a combination of various groups, or loose groupings, representing different emphases of political commitment.

- *Holdovers of the Brezhnev Politburo*. This may be a very small group with only Gromyko and Shcherbitsky, in addition to Gorbachev himself. But it would probably be incorrect to call these people "Brezhnevites": Shcherbitsky has ruled in the Ukraine longer than most Western observers expected, but for reasons which do not necessarily have much to do with Brezhnev nostalgia. Gromyko is more representative of such a mood, and he has become a spokesman for the frustrations of the old generation. But while nostalgia for the past exists at a lower level, a realignment has taken place at the top. At least those who would dare to accept unconditionally the past heritage would be a tiny and self-defeating minority.

- *True Gorbachev supporters*. One can safely put into it Alexandr Yakovlev, promoted full Politburo member last June as the most articulate spokesman of *perestroika* and *glasnost*; foreign Minister Eduard Shevardnadze and probably Viktor Nikonov, the party secretary in charge of agriculture. Other members of the same group hold top jobs but are still outside of the hard core of the leadership. Such members include defence minister Dmitri Yazov; Party secretary Anatoli Lukyanov; and first deputy prime minister, Vsevolod Murakhovsky; before his dismissal alternate Politburo member and first secretary of the Moscow party, Boris Yeltsin, also belonged to this category. These political leaders have been associated with Gorbachev in the past, have advocated some of his contested ideas, or have clearly been promoted with his protection.

- *Politburo members critical of, indifferent, or opposed to, Gorbachev's policies* -- who could most appropriately be called "Andropovian." They include two leaders promoted to the Politburo during the brief tenure of Andropov, between November 1982 and February 1984 (Mikhail Solomentsev and Vitali Vorotnikov), but also several others who, while having reached Politburo status later, had their main promotion during the same period. These are Yegor Ligachev, appointed chief of the party cadres' department and secretary in 1983; Nikolay Ryzhkov, chief of government today, but selected by

Andropov in 1983 to become Party secretary in charge of economy; Nikolai Slyunkov, who holds the some job today, promoted in 1983 to become head of the Party in Belorussia; Lev Zaikov, another secretary in charge of defence industry, selected by Andropov in 1983 to replace Romanov in Leningrad; Viktor Chebrikov, KGB chairman since 1982; altogether seven full Politburo members, a majority of this body.

While it is impossible to assess the views of all the thirteen members on every specific issue one can assume that the main political cleavages broadly correspond to these three categories. Basically everybody agrees that Brezhnevite stagnation cannot be allowed to continue and that changes have to be made. There is certainly an overwhelming majority in favor of discipline and the corresponding campaigns already begun under Andropov -- against alcoholism, shoddy workmanship, absenteeism, corruption and negligence. There is probably also a majority to support economic reform despite the many differences as to modality. Thus, *perestroika* has become the generally accepted frame of reference. But some political leaders have a narrow conception of it; others support the principle of *perestroika* but are against it in practice.

In this respect, Gorbachev is certainly as "Andropovian" as any other, but he has added to the legacy of the first of Brezhnev's successors a contribution of his own: democratization and openness. And this new feature is the one which creates problems, not only with "Brezhnevian" holdovers but also with some of the "Andropovians".

One major indication of this became visible in the second half of 1986. This is when Gorbachev, after the meagre results of "his" first party congress and the campaign for restructuring of the economy and society, moved towards more democracy and *glasnost*, lifted the ban on the media, and launched an appeal to the cultural "front" against the apparatus. The difficulty of convening the CC plenum on cadres policy, which took place in January 1987 only after at least three postponements, clearly had its origin in the Politburo, the only body which is entitled to decide such matters. The same can be said about the discrepancies between Gorbachev's report and the CC resolution, also written by the Politburo and CC secretariat. The backlash in the following months from conservative spokesmen was in all likelihood also encouraged at Politburo level.

A special case has to be made here about Yegor Ligachev. Ligachev was clearly number two in the Party in the first two years of Gorbachev's rule, in fact, for several months up to the party congress the only "supersecretary", i.e. a CC secretary occupying simultaneously a seat as full member of the Politburo. He himself was to confirm his special status in the power hierarchy when he revealed in an interview in Paris in December 1987 that it is not the General Secretary but he, Ligachev, who "is chairing the meetings [of the CC secretariat], and at the request of the Politburo of the Central Committee, organising its work."[14] Older than Gorbachev by eleven years he began a career under Stalin which never crossed Gorbachev's path. His election to the Politburo as early as April 1985 was probably due to the preference by Chernenko's supporters to have an "experienced" and "reliable" party leader at the side of the young new General Secretary. He has taken a tough line against corruption and alcoholism, and in many instances demonstrated orthodox ideological inclinations. His advocacy of market reforms in the economy is either non-existent or at best guarded. He has failed to support Gorbachev's proposals for multi-candidate elections of lower and middle-level party officials. He rallied behind the old generation by his praise of the Stalinist past, including the 1930's. A speech he made along those lines in March 1987 was instantly used as a point of reference by conservative speakers at the Russian Soviet Federated Socialist Republic (RSFSR) writers' meeting in the same months at which one speaker compared the new state of affairs in the cultural sphere to the July 1941 retreat of Soviet forces in front of the "barbarians" and called for a "new Stalingrad". Ligachev has clearly emerged as an alternative option for the position of General Secretary, and as an advocate of a -- to the traditionalists -- more amenable version of *perestroika*.

He may have suffered a setback in June 1987 when Alexandr Yakovlev, already junior CC secretary since March 1986, received full Politburo status. His is clearly different platform in Ligachev's very field of ideology. A comparison of statements by both men over the past years unquestionably shows that Yakovlev advocates a much more liberal approach to *glasnost* and democracy, a more market oriented approach to economic reform and also a greater dosage of political reform. He is now much better positioned to become number two. However, the removal of Yeltsin, another outspoken reformist, from the "first circle" of power may have strengthened the conservatives.

Generally speaking the events surrounding the "Rust affair" and the course of the the June 1987 plenum have confirmed that, on the one hand, Gorbachev is very much in control of the levers of power while the subsequent events (e.g. speeches by Chebrikov and Ligachev, the "Yeltsin affair", the activities of Pamyat etc.) demonstrate, on the other hand, that the struggle over power, authority, and the future course of *perestroika* is not over. As at other times of struggle for power in the past (notably in 1957-58 when Khrushchev tried to consolidate his victory over the "anti-party group"), the General Secretary must enhance his power base in the

14 *Le Monde*, December 4, 1987.

secretariat by increasing its weight in the Politburo. Today already six party secretaries, more than at any time under Brezhnev, are now "supersecretaries". But given Ligachev's important role in the secretariat this task may not be easy.

## 3. Society and Bureaucracy: Support for, or Resistance to, Change?

Before Gorbachev's ascendancy to power there were unmistakable signs of a mounting social crisis. Information recently made available in the Soviet Union emphasizes the magnitude of the problems. A tremendous transformation has taken place in Soviet society. The city population has grown by more that 100 millions in 30 years, and the pains are being seen and felt more clearly than ever. One million orphans and abandoned children have to be taken care of by the state, in special homes, or by foster parents. There has been a long period without any increase in life expectancy, even a decline for infants and working-age males. As many as 53 percent of all school children are reported to have impaired health. More than 39,000 Soviet citizens are said to have been killed in one year in traffic-accidents, an enormous figure considering the relatively low number of cars and kilometres driven. The numer of accidents at work are also high. And both types of accident, as well as other social ills, such as absenteeism, abortion, divorce, shoddy workmanship, and disease, are more often than not attributable to one factor whose pervasive influence still has not been significantly curtailed: alcoholism.

On the basis of his own public statements it is evident that Gorbachev is conscious of the full extent of the problem. He is also quite aware that he faces a petrified economic and political system suffering under the lack of free exchange of ideas, open discussion, new impulses form the outside world, and failure to develop talents in economic affairs and in intellectual life. While the party apparatus is geared to administrating the system as it has been inherited from the Stalin era, Gorbachev is now asking the party to initiate and involve itself in a dynamic political process aimed at modernizing and changing the system.

As argued above, for lack of a viable alternative, this drive by and large at present finds its support in the top party leadership, and is very much endorsed by the large majority of the *intelligentsiya*. At the middle and lower levels of the party, conservatism and braking mechanisms are more pervasive. This applies also to the various layers of the economic bureaucracy, and not surprisingly as plans under discussion envisage a cut of about 40 percent in the bloated administrative apparatus putting at risk the jobs of a major portion of the approximately 16 million state and party officials.[15] Resistance and procrastination by the economic administrators, and by enterprise managers, would be particularlry damaging since they

15 Such plans were revealed by I. Laptev, editor-in-chief of *Izvestiya* in October 1987.

monopolize the knowledge needed to make the system work during any period of transition; at the same time genuine economic decentralization and reform in the direction of a market economy would deprive them of a great deal of power and influence.

In order to overcome such difficulties Gorbachev would certainly like to mobilize working class support for the *perestroika*. But this would require measurable improvements which have not, as yet, been delivered. In fact, up to now the average Soviet citizen has seen less the benefits of change than its drawbacks. The latter include reinforcement of discipline, the struggle against alcoholism, and repression of "non labor incomes". New quality controls in the factories have brought about a reduction of bonuses for workers and in its wake protests, disorders and strikes. Altogether *glasnost* and *perestroika* have not been popular among the workers. A possible exception to this picture may be the peasants who have already made certain gains with the enhancement of the private plot and the encouragement of autonomous "brigades" in the collective farms.

Nationalism in non-Russian areas is also a potential focus for opposition, and the more so since nationality policy seems up to now to be a weak point of Gorbachev's policies. With the backing of Ligachev Moscow has extended the practice of moving cadres from one Soviet republic to another. This has brought about the appointment of more Russians in non-Slavic areas and at least in one case provoked a riot: in Alma-Ata in Kazakhstan in December 1986. Furthermore, a renewed emphasis on the teaching in Russian language has antagonized nationalist feelings while the more objective approach of history has stimulated national intellectuals to question the policy of repression and forced assimilation under Stalin and after. The effects of this can be gauged in the Crimean tartars' protests, the demonstrations which occurred in the Baltic republics in August 1987 and the greater assertiveness of Muslims in the Central Asian republics. Such problems are not much alleviated by the fact that some of the ethnic conflicts are not necessarily directed against Russians or other Slavs but against other nationalities, as indicated, for instance, in the violent clashes between Armenians and Azeris in February and March 1988 over the, for the most part Christian inhabited, Nagorny-Karabach region in Muslim Azerbaidzhan.

At the same time, the existence of resistance, procrastination and opposition to the policies of *glasnost* and *perestroika* are openly admitted by the Soviet media and by Gorbachev himself, and this is new in the Soviet system. To be sure, opponents are not identified by name, as happened in the 1920s, but their arguments are frequently aired.

Finally, there has been an overlap between a Stalinist type of opposition and a more patriotic, even anticommunist type. In fact, *glasnost* has been used by chauvinistic elements to push forward, notably through the channel of the "Pamyat" association, highly reactionary and antisemitic views. The same circles could be used by orthododx party elements to discredit *glasnost* but also to put obstacles in the way of a détente-oriented foreign policy.

All these actual and potential sources of opposition do not escape the attention of the police and its numerous informers. That may explain what seems to be a change of attitude of the KGB towards Gorbachev and his policies. The KGB was clearly allied with Gorbachev at the beginning of his tenure for his having supported Andropov's policies. Chebrikov, the KGB chief appointed by Andropov, is rumored to have strongly backed the new party leader against his rival Grishin at the time of Chernenko's death, and most likely as a result was made a full Politburo member a month later.

Since that time, however, there have been signs of a change. To be mentioned in this context is the Daniloff affair in the summer of 1986 which took place precisely at a point in time when Gorbachev was planning to attend the Reykjavik summit; the death in jail of Marchenko when Gorbachev had decided to free a number of dissidents; and unpleasant rumors about Gorbachev's wife Raisa, including the reported circulation of a video film about her behaviour abroad. Also rumours about an alleged attempt against the life of the General Secretary in the summer of 1986 may have been spread by the same organization with the idea to be conveyed that *glasnost* and *perestroika* would not outlive their main architect and that, hence, it would be risky to associate oneself with the new line.

The relationship between Gorbachev and the military is particularly sensitive and significant, and hence deserves separate treatment.

## 4. Civil-Military Relations: Threat to Gorbachev's Power?

When Gorbachev assumed power in March 1985 he inherited a rather tense relationship between the party leadership and the armed forces. Since then he has adopted some measures to lessen the internal conflict but taken others which could reignite it.

The tension between the armed forces and the party in the late 1970s and early 1980s probably had its origins in several distinct but interrelated issues. The invasion of Afghanistan, the failure of the Soviet armed forces to subdue that country, and the effect of the protracted operation on East-West relations and world opinion in all likelihood led to mutual recrimination as to who was to blame.

In January 1981, President Reagan was inaugurated, and he launched a major build-up in American military strength across the board, of which the announcement of the Strategic Defence Initiative (SDI) in March 1983 was of particular significance. At the same time Soviet military leaders were dismayed by the failure of Soviet diplomats to negotiate the cancelation of NATO's decision to deploy Pershing II and cruise missiles in response to the growing arsenal of SS-20s in the Western part of the Soviet Union and in implementation of the perceived need to acquire selective nuclear employment options.

Next was the uncertainty of the elderly Soviet party leaders in the early 1980s as to how to deal with severe setbacks to the SALT/START negotiating process, thus for all practical purposes putting an end to Soviet hopes to limit and reduce the nuclear competition in the strategic and intercontinental field.

Another source of controversy was doctrinal. Whereas Brezhnev, at the 26th CPSU congress in 1981, had renounced the idea of victory in nuclear war Ogarkov, for several years, continued to cling to it -- even though he too questioned the wisdom of an accelerated nuclear arms race. His primary concern, however, was the competition in high-technology conventional arms.

Finally, it must have been extremely worrying for the professional military officers that the party seemed incapable of effectively countering the economic decline and making sure that the USSR, in the 1990's would be able successfully to compete with the United States in all spheres of military technology.

It was apparently in this situation of deteriorating civil-military relations that Marshal Ogarkov pointed to increasing military threats and demanded *additional* resources and authority to enable him to handle the effective breakdown of the SALT process and the necessary response to the new American strategic forces and to SDI -- in addition to the resources needed for the on-going modernization of the theatre forces. At a meeting chaired by Brezhnev in October 1982 and on other occasions he was told that he was receiving all the means he required for both these tasks. Ogarkov, however, still seemed to be dissatisfied and continued to press his arguments before Brezhnev's successors, Andropov and Chernenko -- to no avail.

Eventually, in September 1984, Ogarkov was removed from Moscow, and from the posts of chief of the General Staff and first deputy minister of defence. His fall from power, however, was not complete. He was sent to head a new high command covering the Western TVD in Western Russia and the Warsaw Pact's northern tier.

Gorbachev thus inherited a tense state of affairs in civil-military relations. Probably because of his still rather weak domestic political power and in clear recognition of the importance of continued military support, a sort of "truce" emerged between the political leadership and the military in 1985 and in some instances carrying over into 1986: For the time being the military retained most of the officers in the existing high command, then headed by the Minister of Defence, Marshal Sokolov. The party seems to have decided at its congress in February-March 1986 not to cut defence spending.

Gorbachev deferred to the military over his plan to withdraw six regiments from Afghanistan in 1986; in the event, only four were removed. Marshal Ogarkov and the other TVD Commanders-in-Chief retained their posts. Gorbachev gave his support to the re-equipment of the armed forces with the newest technology and approved the continued modernization of the theatre forces -- though with some amendments in the organizational field. And he relieved the armed forces of some of the burdens of *glasnost* to the borne by other elements of Soviet society.

Army-party tensions seemed to lessen. But as time progressed and the pace of change in Soviet politics and society quickened the "truce" began to dissolve. Most important are the following developments.

- After the CC plenary meeting in January 1987 Party control over the military has more strongly been reasserted, and some of the measures taken have a clearly symbolic and demonstrative character.

- Demands for *perestroika* in the armed forces have become more insistent.

- The military is no longer exempted from harsh criticism concerning internal discipline and morale, performance in training and exercises, and use of economic resources.

- In personnel policy the rate of turnover has accelerated. Gorbachev has brought into the vacant positions in the Defence Council -- basically the Politburo in defence sessions with the party chief in the chair -- new members of his own choice and persuasion. G.V. Romanov, a full member of the Politburo and CC secretary responsible for the arms industry and one of Gorbachev's main rivals, was removed from power in July 1985. He has replaced many senior military leaders including S.G. Gorshkov (navy), V.F. Tolubko (strategic rocket forces), V. Petrov (army and first deputy minister of defence), P.S Kutakhov (air force), A. Altunin (civil defence), and A.A. Yepishev (Main Political Administration).

- The defence minister is no longer simultaneously a full member of the Politburo: After Ustinov's death in 1984 Marshal Sokolov remained a candidate member (while V.M. Chebrikov, the chief of the KGB was been accorded full membership), and so does his successor, General Yazov.

- In the aftermath of the "Rust affair" at the end of May 1987, Marshal Sokolov was ousted.[16] The commander-in-chief of the Soviet Air Defence Forces, Marshal A. Koldunov, was replaced. Several other air defence officers were demoted and expelled from the party's ranks. Most painful for the military establishment's pride and a declaration of "no confidence" in a whole generation of senior military leaders was the bypassing of all the likely contenders for the office of defence minister (e.g. Akhromeyev, Lushev, Kulikov and - of course - Ogarkov) and the appointment of a general from the second echelon of the military hierarchy: General Yazov.

- The previous, demonstratively privileged, position of the military in Soviet society and politics has been scaled down. At important celebrations, starting from party leader Chernenko's funeral in February 1984, the senior military figures atop the Lenin mausoleum have been shunted to a less prominent position than in previous decades; their numerical presence at such occasions has been curtailed. The armed forces, which had always been named at a prominent place in the rank ordering of appeals at the occasion of the celebrations for the October revolution, have been relegated to the lower end.

- Finally, Gorbachev has partly allowed and partly initiated a discussion of international security and military doctrinal affairs pointing in the direction of a complete revision of well established strategic thought and military postures. The importance of economic factors in "correlation of forces" for the conduct of Soviet foreign policy is being stressed;[17] nuclear weapons are to be abolished; "sensible" or "reasonable" sufficiency is to replace "equal security"; and strategic conventional defence is to have precedence over offence.

Such trends, however useful for foreign policy and propaganda purposes some of which may be, are clearly of concern to traditional military officers; their latent dissatisfaction and resistance is certainly one of the factors which lessen the chances of a comprehensive reform process.

---

16 On the "Rust affair" see above, ch. III, sect. 3.

17 See below, ch. V, sect. 1.

## 5. Summary

The processes of change in Soviet domestic politics are by no means complete. Their direction is still unclear and controversial. They will most likely not proceed, therefore, in a consistent fashion. Forward movement will probably be interrupted by setbacks. At this point one can only submit the following, tentative, conclusions.

Gorbachev is indeed a reformer, much more so than Andropov and Khrushchev, and on a broader front, with the calls for democratization and *glasnost* being added to the demands for discipline and economic modernization. These are trends and not yet accomplished facts. But the trends are in the right direction for if changes can make the Soviet system viable they would have to be along the lines as currently drawn.

Gorbachev is an efficient and able leader, persistent and dynamic, and determined to use to the fullest extent his prerogatives as Secretary General and the important right of initiative that goes with this position. In other words, he should not be underestimated. While tremendous obstacles remain he might succeed.

He will nevertheless have to solve along the path crucial contradictions. After an initial period of *perestroika*, which will probably end in 1990 or 1991, the contradictions may become more acute, and opposition more vigorous. He may then have to choose between greater realism and the optimism he is proclaiming, as well as betweeen the further extension of the reform programme on the one hand and the cohesion of the Soviet Union and the Soviet empire in Eastern Europe on the other.

# *V. Soviet Foreign Relations: "New Thinking" -- and Behavior?*

## 1. Changes in Ideology

As with most other countries which have embarked on major domestic change, including Russia after the Bolshevik revolution, foreign policy in the Soviet Union under Gorbachev is an area where continuity is the rule rather than the exception. In fact, given the strategic and geopolitical position of the Soviet Union and its role as a superpower, the current Soviet leader will most likely pursue objectives and goals similar to those adhered to by his predecessors.

Yet whereas *perestroika* in domestic affairs is condemned to be a slow and painful process, change in foreign policy could be rapid. The number of personnel involved in a *perestroika* of foreign affairs is more limited, the intensity of vested interests lower and the power of the constituencies potentially affected less formidable than in domestic affairs. Thus it would have been surprising if the new dynamism and the demands for "radically" new solutions to old problems in the domestic sphere would not have found their counterpart in foreign policy. And indeed they have.

They have above all affected the very basis of the Soviet conduct in international affairs: Marxist-Leninist ideology.

The "erosion", and even the "end of ideology" have been predicted time and again. But time and again its strength and relevance for Soviet foreign policy have remained unbroken. What did change at crucial junctures of history, however, was the *meaning* and *content* of ideology, and sometimes merely the *emphasis* given to its individual components.

But in general the direction into which such shifts have pointed was away from orthodoxy, rigidity and antagonism to a more benign and cooperative inflection of "peaceful coexistence". This is precisely the direction into which Gorbachev's calls for a "new political thinking" in international relations are aiming. It is also encouraging for the West since without ideological transformation all the changes in Soviet foreign policy will most likely remain tactical. Change in goals presupposes reformulation of the dogma.

When looking at the current -- acutual or incipient -- shifts in ideology it is important to realize that they are often internally inconsistent. Not all of them are new, some of them were developed under Brezhnev. Not all of the reformulations and reinterpretations have authoritative backing. While some authors may express the convictions of the reformist wing in the Soviet leadership, others may deviate from any realistically conceivable consensus in the Politburo and Central Committee. Obviously, such difficulties of interpretation are generic in the current conditions of *glasnost*. With these reservations in mind, what *are* the most important actual or incipient "creative adaptations" of ideology, and notably of the theory of "peaceful coexistence"? What new concepts of international security are taking, or seem to take, shape?

First, *the traditional interpretation of "peaceful coexistence" as a special form of class struggle is being deemphasized.* Universal problems are said to exist and to require common solutions, foremost among them survival and the avoidance of nuclear war. To that extent ideological reformulation is beginning to stress the priority of peace over the class struggle. In addition, as Gorbachev stated at the 27th party congress, there are numerous other common problems which need to be addressed: radioactive fallout from nuclear-reactor accidents, depletion of natural ressources, destruction of the environment, poverty, hunger, and overpopulation.

In the past, as Soviet theoreticians now admit, emphasis in the practical policies of the socialist countries was usullay "not put on the common, human but the social, class-based aspects". Today they recognize more than before the "dialectics of the mutual relationship between the one and the other".[18]

Second, quite related to the principle of universality is the idea of *interdependence* -- also a Western concept which used to be anathema to Soviet ideologists but which is now beginning to enter the Soviet vocabulary and erode the principle of "irreconcileable antagonism". In line with the emphasis on interdependence, international security has been acknowledged by Gorbachev, at the 27th party congress and thereafter, to be indivisible. In his view no country could hope to achieve it at the expense of the other. Only mutual security could realistically be aimed for. (This is what the West German social democrats meant when they developed the idea of *"Sicherheitspartnerschaft"* -- partners in security matters.)

But the new inflection of "peaceful coexistence" remains ambiguous. Yakovlev, for instance, has stated that "the concept of an interrelated world and the need for the cooperation of all humanity does not reduce by one iota the problems of ideological antagonism between socialism and capitalism".[19] Kurt Hager, the chief East German party ideologist, even speaks of a "sharpening of the ideological struggle between socialist and bourgeois ideology".

This apparent (to the uninitiated bourgeois scholar probably real) conceptual problem is dialectically dissolved by the traditional distinction between the social and class nature of the two opposed systems and the "obsolescence" of capitalism on the one hand, and the possibility of their "coexistence" at the political and state level on the other. It is difficult to fathom what this means in practice. If by this is meant that the struggle between the two systems should be one of ideas and of example rather than of political, economic and military rivalry, so much the better. But the suspicion remains that the "ideological" struggle still has a way of spilling over into competition in other fields, including the military. Certainly, generally accepted Soviet interpretation does not go as far as the thesis advocated by Bovin who argues that, politically, capitalism not only had "a right to exist" but that the two "historically irreconcileable" systems, capitalism and socialism, "are forced to cooperate and to *strengthen* each other, in order to survive and continue the controversy".[20]

18 V.V. Zagladin, *Voprosy filosofii*, No. 2 (1986), p. 7.

19 *Vestnik Academii Nauk SSSR*, No. 6 (1987), p. 76.

20 *Das 20. Jahrhundert und der Frieden* (Moscow), No. 9 (1986), p. 4 (emphasis supplied).

A third change in the ideological underpinning of Soviet foreign policy is the idea that *security in the nuclear age "cannot be safeguarded by military-technical means alone"*; that the achievement of security "is also a political task"; and that this task could not be achieved "from positions of strength". Previously the concept of the "correlation of forces" was an important, or perhaps even the most important operational principle on which Soviet foreign policy was "scientifically" based. Thus, under Brezhnev detente was regarded as being based on a greater degree of realism among the leaders of the imperialist countries, and this attitude in turned was explained as being the result of a "significant shift in the correlation of forces in favour of socialism". As Soviet foreign policy practice showed, this shift was interpreted as being caused primarily by Soviet advances in military power relative to the United States and Western Europe.

Contrary to much evidence that the growth in Soviet military power had evoked a corresponding response in the West and had, particularly in the United States, hardened attitudes towards the Soviet Union, Andropov and Chernenko continued to labour -- and suffer -- under Brezhnevite operational principles. Today, however, the notions that it is socialist strength that induces capitalist restraint, and that peace is the more stable the stronger the camp of socialism, can no longer be found in authoritative Soviet sources.

A fourth change was introduced by Gorbachev at the 27th party congress where he proclaimed that *war in the nuclear age war were "inadmissible" (nedopustimyi).* Then and in other contexts it was clear that he referred to all wars. Taken at face value this would render obsolete all the previous elaborate distinctions between "just" and "unjust" war and their single overriding principle that since the Soviet Union would never conduct an aggressive war, but only defend itself or help other socialist countries defend themselves, any war in which the Soviet Union found itself was to be considered "just".

As with the other new inflections in ideology this reinterpretation of "just" and "unjust" war is contradicted by current assertions to the effect that "Marxists are not pacifists; they regard the just [wars], the defensive and national liberation wars, as natural and in accordance with the laws of development *(zakonomernyi)*".[21]

A fifth development in ideology worth noting are new assessments concerning the *nature of imperialism*. Not only do some of the current Soviet leaders and analysts find capitalism more resilient than did most of their predecessors. More important than that is the fact that some of them no longer regard "imperialism", i.e. according to Lenin, capitalism "at its highest stage", as inherently and irrevo-

21 V. Afanasev, *Pravda*, December 5, 1986.

cably "agrressive" and attempting to solve internal structural crises by "militarism". Gorbachev, in his speech at the 70th anniversary of the October revolution, did not go as far as that but he did at least pose the question as to whether the Leninist assumptions were still valid in this respect.

Such hesitation to discard traditional Lenininst notions is important to bear in mind. For if "imperialism", as stated in the revised CPSU programme and the main documents of the 27th party congress, is still "aggressive" by the very nature of its existence and the chief source of war, "peaceful coexistence" will continue to have limited scope in Soviet foreign policy. Such hesitation of the party leader on this and other ideological issues also underlines the fact that the processes of ideological adaptation and change are far from complete. There is so far no explicit statement as to what was wrong with the "old thinking". There is still ambiguity as to the precise status of the world revolutionary goal of "universal communism" and to whether this goal has been abandoned or continues to be a guiding operational principle for Soviet foreign policy. How much "active struggle" to achieve this goal and "help along history" is legitimate? Some isolated exceptions notwithstanding, all the "antagonisms" are still considered to be operative: social, intra-state, interstate and transnational, as well as those between the "three power centres of imperialism" (the United States, Western Europe and Japan), and between socialism and capitalism.

But even though the processes of ideological change are incomplete and do not, from the Western perspective, go far enough to alleviate suspicion, they are aiming in the right direction. To some extent they are perhaps even now capable of establishing interrelationships with the conduct of the Soviet Union in world affairs.

## 2. Shifts in Strategy, Tactics, and Personnel

What is it, then, that is new in Soviet foreign policy? What has changed is, first, the *relationship between domestic and foreign policy*. Today the primacy of the former over the latter seems well established. In the detente period Brezhnev had attempted to evade major domestic reform, foremost in economic affairs, by utilizing Western credit, technology and know-how, and simultaneoulsy by a militarily-oriented, expansionist foreign policy. The glories of globalism were apparently meant to divert attention from the deficiencies of Soviet internal development. Gorbachev and his advisors are more conscious of the fact that improvement of Soviet economic performance must primarily be an indigenous effort, and that overextension and overcommitment abroad can not only be costly and risky but also detract from this effort. They also apparently hope to improve the image and influence of the Soviet Union in world affairs as a result of successful domestic transformation.

Gorbachev is most likely quite consicious of the fact that the relationship between domestic and foreign policy can work also in the opposite direction. Since the beneficial effects of *perestroika* will be visible, if at all, only in the medium or long term, success in the improvement of the Soviet Union's prestige and power abroad can alleviate some of his domestic problems, i.e. the more progress he can make in Soviet-American arms control and crisis management, and generally "making peace more secure", the more secure will be his own domestic position.

Second, as in interal affairs, *past failures and present realities are more realistically taken into account*. The majority of the present Politburo members experienced in 1983-84 what can probably be called the worst international isolation of the Soviet Union since the 1920s. Brezhnev and Andropov failed to forestall, or at least delay or modify, the stationing of intermediate-range nuclear forces (INF) in Western Europe. Their policies of diplomatic pressure, and political and military "countermeasures" had produced a narrowing of differences between the "three main power centres of imperialism", as well as increasing trends of security cooperation between these centres and China. Obviously a new approach was needed to put the Soviet Union back into the international game.

Third, as in domestic politics, *the skill and sophistication of the foreign policy makers has improved*.

- On the surface Andrei Gromyko made a formidable impression with his long time competence and self-confidence, developed to a degree of megalomania in the last years of Brezhnev's tenure and especially under Chernenko. But he lacked imagination, flexibility and even scope, as witnessed by his nearly complete disinterest for Africa, Latin America, and a large part of Asia. These areas were covered by the international department of the CC. Its long-time chief, Boris Ponomarev, however, had looked at these parts of the world mainly through ideological lenses.

- The most influential members of the new foreign policy making elite in the Politburo and the CC are former diplomats and scholars. Many of them are *Amerikanisty*, specialists on American affairs. Foremost among them are Anatoly Dobrynin, former ambassador to the United States, who is secretary of the Central Committee responsible for relations with non-communist countries but, as his visit to Kabul with foreign minister Shevardnadze in January 1987 showed, also actively involved in policy towards communist states as long as the matter at hand concerns US-Soviet relations; Georgi Kornienko, a former first deputy foreign minister and previously Dobrynin's right hand in Washington, who is now his (Dobrynin's) new deputy in the Central Committee; Yuli Vorontsov, former deputy ambassador in Washington, who has succeeded Kornienko in the foreign ministry and Viktor Karpov in his post as chief negotiator at the arms talks in Geneva; and Aleksandr Bessmertnykh, also a former deputy ambassador to Washington, who is a deputy foreign minister.

- In addition, the former Soviet ambassador to Canada, Aleksandr Yakovlev, has been elevated to the post of secretary of the Central Committee responsible for propaganda and, since June 1987, to full membership of the Politburo.
- One of the most visible experts in the field, Georgi Arbatov, remains in the post as director of the Institute for the United States and Canada.

As is particularly evident in the case of Yakovlev and Arbatov, the impressive array of *Amerikanisty* in important positions does not mean that Soviet policies are bound to move in a pro-American direction. What it does mean, however, is that the relationship with the United States is seen by Gorbachev as the main issue in Soviet foreign relations. It also means that the advice he receives is more professional, less dogmatic and ideological.

Fourth, the new team of foreign policy makers seems more *conscious of the erosion of the effectiveness of traditional instruments* in Soviet policy toward the West. As far as one is able to establish, they realize better than their predecessors that the communist parties are of dubious value when it comes to influencing Western government policy. They are certainly conscious of the fact that the strength of the "peace movement" in Western Europe has waned. They are, therefore, more prepared to deal with such forces as are representative of the political mainstream in the West, above all and preferentially, the social democratic parties, but also the liberals and the conservatives.

Fifth, the *costs, benefits, and risks of expansionism in the Third World* are seen in a different light today than in the 1970s. In the Brezhnev period, the dispatch of military advisers and arms, and the cooperation with "proxies", such as Cuba and Vietnam, seemed to have brought about substantial gains at little risk of confrontation with the United States. However, the subsequent years began to look different as the adversary superpower gave the impression that it had overcome the Vietnam and Watergate syndromes and was ready to oppose more vigorously the USSR worldwide.

The success of Soviet and Cuban intervention in Angola and Ethiopia had turned out to be less than straightforward; continued Soviet support and Cuban military involvement were required to prevent deteriorating conditions from leading to a collapse. Vietnam's victory in the south of the country and its occupation of Cambodia had brought about not only economic costs but also political difficulties, complicating Sino-Soviet relations and the relationship between the USSR and the Association of Southeast Asian Nations (ASEAN). Finally, the Soviet intervention in Afghanistan had not, as some Soviet political and military leaders may have originally thought, led to a rapid decrease in guerilla activity. It remained, as Gorbachev deplored at the 27th Party Congress, an "open wound".

Thus, to reduce the economic "costs of empire", contain the political repercussions over relations with the United States and other countries, and lessen the risk of counterintervention or counterrevolution supported by the Reagan administration, the Gorbachev leadership seems to consider it appropriate to avoid new commitments -- above all new *military* involvements. At the same time it is still clinging to most of the global positions gained by its predecessors, attempting to consolidate those gains and making them less risky and costly.

Examples of the former aim (avoidance of new commitments) is evident in Nicaragua and South Africa, where Moscow has adopted a low profile. Until the autumn of 1986, one example of the latter (safeguarding the positions reached) had been Afghanistan. Since then Gorbachev has steered a more or less consistent course towards withdrawal of Soviet forces, attempting to extricate the Soviet Union at minimum cost.

In fact, given its considerable importance for Soviet domestic and foreign policy, as well as for Western perceptions and the course of East-West relations, Gorbachev's *decision to withdraw Soviet troops from Afghanistan* must be regarded as a sixth major indication of change.

Irrespective of whether the decision to withdraw should be interpreted as sufficent proof for Soviet "new thinking" or a necessary tactical retreat, the taking of the decision itself presents ample evidence for the determination with which a policy change, once decided upon, is put into practice. It also serves to show that it is wise, in the Gorbachev era, not to dismiss lightly harbingers of change.

Indications of a change in policy since the autumn of 1986 had been plentiful. (1) Soviet aides had been saying that the invasion of Afghanistan was a mistake. (2) In the reporting of events Soviet losses and costs were being emphasized rather than success and actual or potential benefits. (3) Writers who, in the past, had glorified Soviet-Afghan cooperation were claiming that the regime in Kabul had reneged on the agreements and commitments under which the USSR had consented to intervene. (4) Even more strongly than in the past, Soviet political leaders and propagandists had asserted that Afghanistan was not a socialist country and did not belong to the "socialist commonwealth". (5) In letters to the central newspapers readers had been allowed to state that the support to the Kabul regime could not be compared to the Great Patriotic War. (6) In public opinion polls, carried out by Soviet and joint Soviet-Western polling organizations, a majority of Soviet citizens was reported as favouring a withdrawal of troops from Afghanistan. (7) In what was reminiscent of the preparation for the US withdrawal from Vietnam and the "Vietnamization" of the war, Soviet and Afghan spokesmen had deemphasized the role played by the Soviet armed forces; they were asserting instead that the Afghan army had grown in strength and effectiveness, and were able to survive a Soviet pullout. (8) Soviet party and government officials, starting in early 1988, began to say publicly that the removal of Soviet troops from Afghanistan depended neither on the conclusion of an international agreement nor on the composition of the government to be left behind.

The Soviet leaders, or at least some of them, apparantly have not given up hope that the Marxist-Leninist regime left behind, once withdrawal begins, will survive. They are still keeping that option open by inisting on their "legitimate right" to continue to supply weapons to what they officially still consider to be a rightful government in Kabul. They have, consequently, steadfastly refused to deal directly with the mudjaheddin.

But this should not detract from appreciating the significance of the Geneva agreement of April 1988 and the Soviet withdrawal in accordance with its provisions. Militarily, Moscow was under no immediate pressure to pull out of Afghanistan but the Soviet armed forces were unable to implement the task set for them. In that sense, the pullout would be the first major admission of defeat of the Soviet armed forces since World War II. It would be an indication of an awareness of the Soviet leadership that there are limits to the benefits that can be derived from the use of military force -- a painful lesson that the Germans and Japanese had to learn in World War II and the United States in Vietnam. It would be the first example of abandonment of a regime put in and kept in power by Soviet arms; of a country at the borders of the USSR which is linked with it by a treaty of friendship and cooperation, as well as close economic ties. And notwithstanding the claim that this country was not socialist, withdrawal and its likely consequences would, ideologically, be an important example of the "wheel of history" being turned back. All of these considerations make the withdrawal of forces an important move, and potentially a risky one domestically for the Soviet party leader.

A seventh new element in Soviet foreign policy is the new *flexibility in diplomacy and the attempt to build up a wide network of political contacts*. One of its objectives is to enhance the Soviet Union's diplomatic, political and cultural presence in countries and organizations in which it was hitherto underrepresented or not represented at all. An indication of this policy, at the the international economic level, is the interest Moscow has expressed in joining, in one for or another, the General Agreement on Tariffs and Trade (GATT) and the International Monetary Fund (IMF), and the apparent readiness not only to come to legal agreements but also to some kind of *political* arrangement with the European Community. Indicative of this objective at the level of international security is the payment of $197 million in back dues for the peacekeeping forces it had previously opposed, the pledge to meet its current dues and the interest it has proclaimed in future UN peacekeeping operations, including in Afghanistan.

The new and more flexible tactics can also be observed in various regions.[22] In the wake of a programmatic statement on Moscow's Asian policy in Vladivostok (July 1986), Gorbachev has endeavored to mend his relations with the Chinese leadership. He has moved in one way or another, even if perhaps only symbolically, on all the three points which, the Chinese have claimed, stand in the way of an improvement of Sino-Soviet relations: the Soviet occupation of Afghanistan; the presence of Soviet troops along the Chinese borders, notably in Mongolia; and Moscow's support for the Vietnamese occupation of Cambodia.

As for the Middle East, Moscow has made concessions on the Egyptian debt, leased tankers to Kuwait, acted as mediator for the Palestinians, persuaded Syria to show more moderation, extended feelers to Israel, and consented to a significant increase in the rate of Jewish emigration. In the Iran-Iraq war, without abandoning its traditional support for Iraq, it has sought to improve its relations with Iran and cautiously avoided being drawn into the taking of sanctions.

Eighth, the Soviet leadership has adopted a *new stance on human rights issues*. In contrast to Brezhnev's adamant rejection of any discussion of human rights in the USSR, even on the basis of the Final Act of the Conference on Security and Cooperation (CSCE), as "inadmissible interference in the internal affairs of the socialist countries", Gorbachev has responded to some of the criticism. In his tenure in office the number of exit visas granted to Jewish "refuseniks" and new applicants has increased, and so has the rate of emigration of ethnic Germans. He has adopted a more activist approach in this sphere too and called for the holding of a human rights conference in Moscow. Such measures, as mentioned, are among other things most likely designed to improve the Soviet Union's standing in world politics and to restore some of the lost powers of attraction of the Soviet model.

---

22 For detail on Soviet policy *vis-à-vis* Western Europe and the United States see below, ch. IV, sect. 3.

An final new element in Gorbachev's foreign policy most likely is a *reassessment of the utility of the arms competition, above all, in the nuclear sphere*. In the 1970s it may have appeared to Soviet political leaders and analysts that NATO may still have been economically and technologically prepared, yet no longer *politically* able to keep up with the Warsaw Pact in the arms competition; that, contrary to the preceding three decades, the Western countries were reacting only belatedly and ineffectively to Soviet initiatives; and that they were increasingly putting faith in arms-control negotiations to redress a deteriorating military balance. Thus, through its arms control proposals, the Soviet Union under Brezhnev and Andropov became an active participant in Western security debates. The weight of its arguments in these debates seemed to be rising.

But starting in the late 1970s, these trends could no longer be regarded as unbroken or unbreakable. Defence outlays in the United States had begun to rise sharply. New challenges were issued to the Warsaw Pact in the form of more sophisticated conventional weapons and Reagan's Strategic Defense Initiative. In conjunction with the deployment of intermediate-range nuclear weapons and the resulting capability of NATO to strike at Soviet territory from Western Europe, as well as the on-going US strategic modernization programmes, it was the Soviet Union that was put into a position to react. Furthermore, it had to respond in the field of high technology in which it could compete less easily and effectively. Gorbachev has drawn the appropriate conclusions from such actual and potential developments and adjusted his arms control initiatives accordingly.[23]

3. The "Common House" versus "Atlanticism"

Yet another characteristic feature of Gorbachev's foreign policy is the *emphasis given to the relationship with the United States*. Initially, until the autumn of 1985, it seemed that priority would be given to the European and Japanese connection.

- Thus, even before his formal inauguration as General Secretary, when he visited London in December 1984 at the head of a Soviet parliamentary delegation, he spoke of Europe as "our common house" *(nash obshchii dom)*, implying that the United States, as a trans-Atlantic power, really had no business in that house; that, as a *Pravda* editorial put it, "Washington is a stranger to that house"; and that the European countries hade common interests, in security matters, which needed to be safeguarded.

- Gorbachev, some of his advisors, especially Yakovlev, and theoreticians of reform, like Aleksandr Bovin, have repeatedly asserted that in addition to geo-

23 For detail see below, the sections on conventional and nuclear arms control.

graphy, "Europe" is bound together by "historical ties" and a "common foundation of European culture"; that people on this side of the Atlantic approached detente and the nature and prospects of East-West contacts more seriously and more responsibly; and that, hence, European political standards are superior to those in the United States.

- Yet another claim that has been made is that, even though the Soviet leadership considered a normalization of relations with the United States to be important, it was "not for a single moment forgetting that the world is not limited to that country alone". Such statements, obviously, can be interpreted to mean that if relations with Washington were to develop unsatisfactorily, Moscow had other options which it could pursue.

- Gorbachev has also advocated the expansion of economic contacts between the Council for Mutual Economic Assistance (CMEA) and the European Community, as well as the establishment of official relations between these two organizations. While the Soviet approach is not new, the expression of Soviet readiness (in talks with Italian prime minister Bettino Craxi in May 1985), "to the extent to which the states of the EEC were acting as one single unit ... to search for a common language with them on specific international problems" was unprecedented: Whereas previously, Soviet interest had extended only to regulating economic relations between the two organizations, Gorbachev for the first time has signaled a Soviet interest in coming to some arrangement with the EC at the *political* level.

- Finally, Gorbachev has seemed to view the *Eureka* programme, that is, the effort by the main Western European countries to increase their technological cooperation, as positive and even to hint at some interest in Soviet participation as long as this programme remained confined to civilian research and development.

As if to demonstrate the priority of Soviet-Western European relations, Gorbachev's first visit abroad as party leader was not to Washington but to Paris in October 1985. On that occasion, practically all the themes that had been raised earlier were authoritatively repeated.

However, a privileged relationship with the Western Europe did not materialize. As Gorbachev's proposal during his visit to Paris in October 1985 and his offer to negotiate separately with France and Britain on nuclear weapons showed, the Soviet leadership has not given up its previous preference for utilizing "imperialist contradictions". Soviet spokesmen and scribes have continued to view with unease the processes of vertical and horizontal integration in Western Europe and have vehemently opposed any semblance of military integration, including the recent efforts at French-West German defence cooperation. Nothing has come so far of Gorbachev's hint to establish political links with the European community. Due to Soviet recalcitrance on the West Berlin problem, the establishment of legal and organizational ties between Comecon and the EC has not yet been achieved. Moscow has continued to oppose Austrian membership in the EC.

As for the economic aspects, the volume of Soviet-Western European trade has continuously been falling in the last few years. To a great extent this is, of course, the result of objective conditions, foremost the substantial shortfall in hard currency because of the decrease in the world market price for oil and gas, the depreciation in the value of the US dollar and the low competitiveness of Soviet industrial products. But the substantial cuts in imports from the OECD countries were *deliberate*, reflecting perhaps a Soviet decison not to exceed certain levels of indebtedness and, consequently, not to reach politically undesirable levels of dependence on the West. Furthermore, the reform of the foreign trade apparatus and of the legal machinery in that sphere, including the the laws governing joint ventures, has not been undertaken vigorously enough to provide for the kind of boost necessary to achieve a reversal in the declining Soviet-West European trade pattern.

Any privileged position of Western Europe in Soviet *Westpolitik*, or even a "normalization" of relations, would certainly require special attention to West Germany. However, Soviet relations with this country are no better than with any other Western European state, and perhaps worse. It does seem that it is Bonn rather than Mosow that would like to see, as Gorbachev put it during foreign minister Genscher's visit to to Moscow in July 1986, a "new page" to be opened in the "book of Soviet-West German relations". The stream of high-ranking visitors seems to be almost exclusively one way: President Richard von Weizsäcker visited the Soviet Union in July 1987, the Bavarian prime minister, Franz-Josef Strauß, in December 1987; and the prime minister of Baden-Württemberg, Lothar Späth, in February 1988.

Only after foreign minister Genscher had visited Moscow four times consecutively, once every year since 1984, did his Soviet counterpart finally find the time for a return visit, in January 1988. Similarly, Gorbachev has found it expedient to delay time and again to visit West Germany. Only after chancellor Kohl, like his foreign minister, will have visited Moscow four times in succession since 1983 (the fourth visit to take place in the autumn of 1988) will Gorbachev pay a return visit to Bonn. In the light of these asymmetries of protocol it seems highly unlikely that, as some West German conservatives and isolated neutralists have hoped,

Gorbachev will launch a new initiative on the German problem, and perhaps make an offer for reunification of the two parts of Germany.

To the extent that Western Europe occupies a privileged position in the current design of the new party leader it seems that it continues to be the main *prize* of Soviet foreign policy, not an entity whose autonomy *vis-à-vis* the United States should be encouraged and whose relations with Eastern Europe be expanded. The purpose of Gorbachev's appeals to Western Europe is most likely not to support any new European processes of integration and to try to separate the USA from Western Europe (this could only be a very long-term objective) but to influence, through the Western European connection, the direction of American policies towards the Soviet Union.

In contrast to the lack of conceptual coherence in Gorbachev's approach towards Western Europe and the relative lack failure to give substance to the theme of "Europe, our common house", his policies towards the United States have been consistent, and the Soviet-American relations have much improved. *Amerikanisty*, as mentioned, occupy the most important positions in the Soviet foreign policy apparatus. The main events of the first three years since Gorbachev's ascendancy to power were nuclear arms control negotiations with the United States, the -- by spring 1988 -- 23 working sessions betwewen foreign ministers Shevardnadze and Shultz on arms control, regional conflicts and human rights, and the summit meetings with President Reagan in Geneva, Reykjavik, Washington and -- scheduled for the end of May 1988 -- Moscow. The Soviet approach of extending the dialogue with the United States has continued even though the first summit meeting in 1985 was held according to an American agenda and although the United States subsequently, in 1986-87, adopted uncompromising and unyielding policies that could easily be characterized as "provocative" by critics inside the Soviet Union.

The likely rationales for these policies towards the West are numerous. The first and most simple probably lies in Moscow's claim to superpower status and political equality with the United States. Negotiations with lesser powers at the periphery of the Soviet Union may be useful for a variety of reasons. But only by being seen internationally as being engaged in negotiation with the opposed world power do the assertions of the Soviet leaders that the two countries have "a special responsibility for the destinies of mankind" appear more credible. Since the claim to equal political status is derived from military parity, this very fact also helps explain why arms control has become the driving edge of Soviet policy toward the West.

Another possible reason may be connected with a reevaluation in Moscow of the apparent strength of "contradictions" in the West. Gorbachev may have drawn the logical conculsion from the experience of the early 1980s that it proved impossible to separate the United States from Western Europe and Japan, and that -- to paraphrase Bovin and other Soviet analysts -- the "objective forces" which bind together the three main "power centers of imperialism" are stronger than those which put them at odds with each other.

Yet another rationale, and one possibly explaining above all Gorbachev's reluctance to "open a new page" in Soviet-West German relations, lies in the constraints imposed by the weakness and vulnerability of the Soviet hegemony in Eastern Europe. Given the, as Helmut Sonnenfeldt put it in 1976, "unorganic" Soviet-Eastern European relationship (i.e. a relationship based on military power, repression and the threat of intervention), any major increase in contact between East and West, and notably between East and West Germany, in the "common house" would pose serious problems for the Soviet Union. At least at this stage of *perestroika* domestically in the Soviet Union and in the "socialist community", the free exchange of people and information would most likely lead to a significant increase in Western, and in particular West German, influence in Eastern Europe, and thus to an unacceptable erosion of Soviet control.

4. Eastern Europe

In contrast to Soviet-Western European relations there has been more movement in the relationship between the USSR and Eastern Europe. The Soviet leadership under Gorbachev clearly proceeds from the operating assumption that the Eastern European regimes are not, and cannot be, exact replicas of the Soviet model. Local conditions are heeded by the indigenous establishments and the Moscow party leadership more than before. Most likely, as Gorbachev seemed to acknowledge during his visit in Belgrade in March 1988, the threshold of a putative Soviet military, Brezhnev Doctrine-type intervention in Eastern Europe has been raised. Also, the military and imperial burden, both in terms of stationed troops and hardware, as well as in the form of Eastern European contributions to the maintenance of communist influence in the world, is acutely felt both in the USSR and in Eastern Europe and no longer regarded as an imperative priority which brooks no discussion.

For quite some time, in Eastern Europe active cooperation with the West, above all in the economic field, rather than total *Abgrenzung*, has become an accepted imperative. Western, not Soviet, science and technology are recognized as the standard by which *desiderata* must be measured. Instead of ideologically shielding the Soviet Union, Eastern Europe has been generating reformist behavior. Also, reform communism is an Eastern European, not a Soviet invention. But what is new is that Eastern European reformist theory and practical experience have now begun to interact with the Gorbachev version of change. The novelty of the situation lies in this interaction -- for the first time ever, the change-seeking regimes and populations in Eastern Europe encounter a similarly disposed suzerain -- rather than in the reformist tenets themselves; Eastern European reformers have preached and tested them for decades, and even Western scholars have internalized them as a part of their analysis of the Soviet system. Gorbachev has proven them right in one way of another.

In 1988, Eastern Europe is still in a period of transition from non-reform to reform. The progression remains reversible, more so in some countries than in others. Its future depends, first and foremost, on the survival of the Gorbachev scheme. The process is also uneven.

- Hungary has already approached the outer limit of the system but, instead of boldly crossing it, has to practise retrenchment and austerity.
- Poland would dearly like to use reform to get itself out of its economic misery only to find that reforms do not yield the kind of prompt results that the country desperately needs. Nevertheless, Poland is well advanced in non-economic "reforms", e.g. in ideological pluralism.
- Bulgaria busies itself with the reorganization of pre-reform institutions, an action which has so far promised more chaos than efficiency.
- In Czechoslovakia, the notoriously reform-hostile incumbents profess somewhat improbably to be in the van of grand reformist designs which purportedly differ from those of the Prague Spring in that they will strengthen, not weaken socialism.
- Romania and East Germany, each for its own particular reason, have so far declined to become reformist in the Gorbachevian sense. The GDR is, nevertheless, benefiting from the more auspicious climate to foster its relations with West Germany and to relax its erstwhile repressive policies at home. The feeling about Romania is that the Gorbachevian reformist precepts will serve well as a policy plan for the country's post-Ceausescu era.

In sum, whereas rhetoric, intent and coping with exigencies prevail over decisive action at this stage, the trend toward reform is there.

On the general plane, Gorbachev prefers an Eastern Europe where everybody strives for greater efficiency while not letting things get out of control. He obviously believes that his is the right recipe for improvement; a joint reformist policy throughout the bloc would suit his preferences. It could probably be better supervised than the present diversity of attitudes. Nevertheless, the age-old dilemma between control and viability continues to apply. Gorbachev has been forced to conclude a *modus vivendi* with the client states: he is not forcing the pace of reform in any one Eastern European country unduly; he is not imposing his precepts where they are not wanted; and he has not engineered the downfall of any of the Eastern European leaders. Systemic security and a coordinated foreign policy of the bloc, with Moscow as the leading centre, has been given priority over coordinated and consensually timed reformism. By the same token, the "reconstruction" of CMEA has not even begun and, apparently, there is difficulty in getting an acceptable blueprint on the drawing board.

Economic and technical inadequacy easily represent the greatest hurdle that the USSR and Eastern Europe seek to clear. The non-economic components of *perestroika* are generally used in a utilitarian fashion as instruments to help economic advancement. As things stand now, *perestroika* is about efficiency and effectiveness of communism, not about its "human face", even if a relaxation of the coercive factor has been chosen to constitute a part of the reform-supportive environment.

There are "special cases" in Eastern Europe which merit particular attention but which can only be enumerated here: the progress of German-German relations against the backdrop of reformism in Moscow and, perhaps, in East Berlin; the transcendence by Hungary of the systemic reform limits; the effect of Polish progress either into another societal eruption or toward a workable reform-supportive consensus between the regime, the Church and the democratic opposition; and the nature of government in post-Ceausescu Romania. But they are six problem areas for Gorbachevism in Eastern Europe which belong to a more general framework.

First, *Eastern Europe does not follow the Soviet leader in unison*, either by choice or for objective reasons. Hence, the non-Soviet part of the bloc will continue to face for some time yet a cluster of different, nationally determined problems, and to produce a cluster of different, nationally determined responses to Moscow's "new course". Reform has not so far helped bring the individual Eastern European countries on the same footing. On the contrary, they now differ from each other more than at any time in their common communist history. Unity in Eastern Europe is still a matter of military, political and ideological exigency, not of a singular reformist purpose.

Second, given the heightened awareness of national economic predicaments, the systemic obstacles and the disunity of reformist purpose, the *"socialist economic integration" through CMEA is seen to have become a pie in the sky*. "Direct links" and "joint enterprises" are largely felt to be centrally imposed undertakings that have little to do with the real needs of, and which bring little benefit to, the participants. The recognition must have begun to dawn that joint scientific and technical advancement along the lines of the December 1985 CMEA plan is unrealizable. The moment may come when those in charge will understand that it would be cheaper for everybody if CMEA were abolished. In the meantime, a trimming exercise may well be in the making. The CMEA bureaucracy certainly cannot pass any cost-benfit test; it is vast, expensive and largely for show. Whatever CMEA does, or most of it, oculd be done without that organization, if only economic relations within the bloc were properly commercialized. Gorbachev may well be induced to seek to transform CMEA into a kind of a small international committee with strategic and coordinative functions, rather than maintaining it as the huge machinery to supervise the relatively simple exchange of Soviet raw materials for Eastern European manufactures which it now is.

Third, *Western -- capitalist, democratic -- standards have not been replaced by Soviet reformist desiderata as the yardstick of change.* In Eastern European perceptions, including those of the establishments, the West offers living proof that things can be made to work whereas Gorbachev offers only a modicum of hope which by no means everyone shares. In view of the well-nigh general acceptance of the West's superiority in economic performance and technical achievement, and because of the less confrontational foreign policy now pursued, the West's opportunities in Eastern Europe have widened both in the economic field and in the supportive "human face" enviroment of the *perestroika*.

Fourth, as internal economic pressures continue to mount, the Eastern European regimes are *likely to seek ways to reduce the share of the "costs of empire" imposed by Moscow* on its European glacis. A further lessening of US-Soviet tensions may well lead to the withdrawal of a substantial number of Soviet troops (whose levels there are unnecessarily high) and their equipment from Eastern Europe and to a reduction in Eastern European contributions to the Warsaw Pact and to Soviet-run schemes as, for example, in underdeveloped communist countries on the periphery of the empire. A cost-benefit analysis of the international (military and other) commitments of *Realsozialismus*, as entered into under Soviet leaders from Stalin to Brezhnev, is overdue. But a change downward will obviously not be an easy undertaking.

Fifth, in view of the large measure of ideological underpinning in all communist regimes, *the tension between dogma and change will inevitably grow as reform advances.* Factional collisions between proponents and opponents, or radicals and conservatives, cannot be excluded. Public pressure for a more consistent deviation from conventional Marxism-Leninism is also likely to increase as neighbouring states venture further along the revisionist road than domestic incumbents. Of special note are ideological disputes connected with a freer review of the individual countries' history and with the so-called "blank spots" in their earlier encounter with Moscow's superior communist power.

Sixth, there is a *higher potential for the advancement of reformism in Eastern Europe than in the USSR*, even if it may not look that way in some countries now. In particular, what can be called the "supportive" environment of the Gorbachevian quest for economic efficiency is fraught in Eastern Europe with the risk of a fast and even explosive progress. The Hungarian revolution, the Prague Spring and the Solidarity period in Poland have shown that national emancipation and democratic aspiration tend to play a stronger role in Eastern Europe than economic matters. Hence, the possibility exists that at least some of the Eastern European countries will once again outpace the USSR in the reformist endeavour, and precisely in this non-economic compartment.

Similarly, the ideologically motivated fear of private enterprise is far less ensconsed in Eastern European political thinking than in the Soviet perspectives. Leadership successions are now almost the order of the day, and on occasion that may (but, of course, need not) usher in reformist experiments on a far larger scale than exist now. A conflict between Moscow and Eastern Europe, like those in 1956, 1968 and 1980-81, cannot be excluded in the future. As long as Gorbachev leads the way, he is benign. Will he remain benign if an Eastern European reformist spring blossoms up into a fully-fledged, liberalizing and democratizing summer which leaves the USSR once again behind?

## 5. Arms Control

### a. New Developments

As to other areas of Soviet foreign policy Gorbachev has brought a new impetus and flexibility to East-West arms control negotiations. First, the Soviet party leader has *returned to the complete and comprehensive disarmament theme prevalent under Khrushchev*. In his January 1986 proposal he raised the prospect of a world without nuclear weapons to be achieved in several stages by the year 2000. He has "improved" on Reagan's utopian vision of "making nuclear weapons impotent and obsolete" (through the build-up of space defences) by rejecting the interpositon of an expensive and in his view unworkable intermediate step and suggesting instead to proceed directly to the abolition of offensive nuclear weapons. But in contrast to Khrushchev the new party leader has combined comprehensive disarmament propaganda with speficic arms control proposals -- and agreements of which the December 1987 Washington treaty to remove an entire class of weapons is so far the most important example. New is also the link he has so skilfully construed between the rhetoric of comprehenisve disarmament and the "old", Brezhnevite designs for the establishment of nucler-free weapons zones, notably in Europe.

Second, Gorbachev has *broken entirely new ground on the inspection issue*. For decades the stubborn Soviet refusal to agree to reliable on-site control and verification procedures had been a major stumbling bloc in East-West arms control. Today the principle of inspection has been conceded. New precedents have been set including the following examples.

- At the Conference on Disarmament in Europe (CDE) in Stockholm in 1986 the Soviet Union for the first time consented to on-site inspection of military moves and manoeuvres by foreign observers on Soviet territory.

- In accordance with an agreement between the private National Resources Defense Council (NRDC) and the USSR Academy of Sciences, American scientists installed the first Western monitoring station at a Soviet nuclear test site, near Semipalatinsk in Kazakhstan, in July 1986.

- In September 1987 the Soviet Union again granted scientists associated with the NRDC, but also three members of the US Congress, permission to visit the Soviet nuclear test site in Semipalatinsk. And in November it agreed to allow inspection of its nuclear test sites, and monitoring of several nuclear blasts on its territory in 1988 in an attempt to improve the machinery of the two treaties constraining underground nuclear explosions.

- In September 1987 Moscow agreed to let Democratic representatives of the House of Congress and members of the NRDC visit the phased-array radar installation at Krasnoyarsk in Siberia which in the almost unanimous view of Western academic and government specialists violates the ABM treaty.

- In October 1987 Western diplomats, journalists and defence experts were allowed to visit a chemical weapons complex in Shikhany on the Volga river. (In the preceding year, according to Western journalists, Lieutenant Kuntsevich, the deputy commander of the chemical troops, had insisted that the Soviet Union had *no* chemical weapons.)

- In the talks on a comprehensive ban on chemical weapons in Geneva the Soviet negotiators have been pushing for more stringent on-site inspection at plant level than their American counterparts. This amounts to a complete reversal of positions of the two superpowers in previous negotiations on that issue.

- In the December 1987 treaty on abolition of medium and short-range nuclear systems the Soviet Union agreed to an inspection and control regime of considerable scope. It provides for on-site verification of the data on the number and location of the missiles to be destroyed; control of the destruction of the missiles; and verification that the treaty provisions are being upheld.
- In March 1988 Gorbachev also proposed international inspection of the space programmes of the major powers and to make sure that the arms competition in space would remain limited -- a suggestion that, like many others, is intended to take even more wind out of the sails of SDI.

Third, in line with Gorbachev's reversal concerning on-site inspection the *outlines of more glasnost' in military affairs* are beginning to become visible. In his September 1987 article on problems of international security, for instance, Gorbachev suggested that data should be provided to allow for comparison of defence expenditures.[24] The revelation by deputy foreign minister Petrovksy that the officially published Soviet military outlays do not include major programmes usually contained in the military budgets of other states and the recurrent complaints by Soviet journalists and academic specialists that they cannot rely, or do not have adequate access to, military data could lay the basis for more realistic and detailed Soviet figurers in the future.

Fourth, there have been *some unilateral gestures of restraint* -- some of which perhaps of dubious value. This applies to the (since February 1987 abandoned) moratorium on underground nuclear testing; cutbacks on the SS-20 deployment to facilitate the Washington agreement; and discontinuation of construction work at the Krasnoyarsk radar site.

Fifth, closely related to the new inflections on "peaceful coexistence" and the demands for "new thinking" in international politics are *new military doctrinal discusssions and emerging new concepts of security*. These include the idea, first raised in the West, of "reasonable sufficiency" *(razumnaya dostatochnost')* of military forces, the achievement of security at "lower levels of armament" and, as Gorbachev put it in a speech in Prague in April 1987, "the removal of the imbalance which has arisen in some categories [of weapons] but not, however, through an increase by the side that is behind but by reductions of the side that is ahead."

---

24 *Pravda*, September 17, 1987.

Sixth, potentially even more important for arms control are assertions to the effect that, historically (e.g. in the battle of Kursk in 1943), *strategic conventional defence proved superior and decisive* as against offense and that -- as Colonel-General M.A. Gareyev, deputy chief of the General Staff, asserted -- one of the "main tenets of the military-technical aspect of military doctrine" is its "profoundly defensive direction".[25] Simultaneously, the declared Soviet aim in conventional arms control is to eliminate the possibility of surprise attack, in fact, to reforge and reposition forces so as to achieve a mutual "structural inability to attack", a term first coined by West German social democratic defence experts.

If such doctrinal revisions were to become generally accepted the door could be wide open for major changes in the Soviet force posture in Central Europe which could be effected either unilaterally or through arms control. However, articles on conventional *offence* still predominate, certainly in the military journals. And doubts about the purposes to be pursued by discussion of "defensive defence" are fed by frank admissions, such as the one by deputy foreign minister Petrovsky, that "the very fact of the proclamation of the doctrine alone is having a salutary effect on the climate and situation in the world."[26]

b. Nuclear Arms Control

In nuclear arms control, perhaps more than in any other field, it seems that traditional objectives are being pursued, even though by new methods. Indeed what Gorbachev has had to say on this topic is not always an expression of "new thinking". In his speech in Tula in 1977, for instance, Brezhnev had already renounced the striving for military superiority, including in nuclear forces. In 1979 the Soviet Military Encyclopedia stated that there could be no victory in nuclear war. In 1981 the party leader reiterated this position, and in conjunction with a new doctrinal emphasis on conventional weapons he tabled a plethora of proposals on no-first-use, and on nuclear-free zones in northern Europe, in the Balkans and in Central Europe. Gorbachev, in turn, has declared that nuclear weapons cannot win a war and should accordingly not be used. He has put this weight behind a wide variety of arms control and disarmament proposals to the West whose main theme is the reduction and ultimate elimination of nuclear weapons from the arsenals of both sides.

It is likely that Gorbachev has accepted the historical argument that the only threat to the Soviet regime and its political system is total defeat and "breakdown" in war, and that the only forces which are capable of inflicting such a measure of

25 *Moscow TV* news conference, June 22, 1987.

26 *TASS*, June 22, 1987.

defeat on the Soviet Union are the nuclear forces of the United States and other NATO countries. The limitation, reduction and, if possible, ultimate removal of such weapons from the armed forces of both sides must be, according to this view, the most urgent task of Soviet foreign policy to be achieved by diplomacy, propaganda and subversion. The Soviet armed forces must, of course, retain, while nuclear weapons exist, the capability to use them and to negate NATO's "flexible response"; they must also have the capacity to inflict "immediate and crushing retaliation" on the enemy, and with restrictions on the means employed. But Gorbachev appears to have decided on the "general line" of the removal of nuclear weapons of all types as his long-term goal, and is visibly moving in that direction. Such a doctrine also reinforces the conviction of the traditional as well as of the more modern oriented alignments in the military establishment that the Soviet Union must always be able to put conventional forces in the field which, in fire power, mobility and size, would be more than a match for any non-nuclear forces that NATO could deploy.

What makes Gorbachev different from his predecessors is that, in 1987, he was willing to pay a price for the achievement of this goal. In the December 1987 Washington treaty he, for all practical purposes, agreed to accept the original American single "zero-zero" option for the withdrawal of the SS-20 intermediate-range missiles from Europe -- without any quantitative or qualitative restriction on the British and French nuclear systems. He also agreed to the destruction of the shorter-range nuclear missiles, the SS-12 and SS-23. He acceded to the US proposal for a broadening of the originally European scope of a prospective "double zero" solution to the global level. Finally, as mentioned, the Soviet leadership agreed to comprehensive verification. In the strategic field, the proposal of 50% cuts in ballistic missiles is on the table, and agreement on this issue no longer seems to be out of reach since Soviet negotiators have -- to gain acceptance of this proposal -- hinted at even more flexibility on SDI.

Ogarkov and other high-ranking officers, both prior to and after Gorbachev's political ascendancy, also have argued that nuclear war cannot be managed. They, too, have questioned the utility of nuclear weapons and urged, first, the necessity of removing the nuclear threat to the USSR and, second, giving more resources to the modernization of Soviet conventional weapons. These two themes are of course linked: reductions in nuclear arms would not diminish or threaten Soviet security, and might even release resources for conventional weapons; conversely, reductions in the former category of weapons would reinforce Soviet advantages in the latter.

It does appear, then, that Gorbachev's assessment of security issues has led him, initially, to aim for maximum benefits for the Soviet Union from the removal of nuclear weapons and -- in due course -- the construction of a non-nuclear, conventional force balance between East and West. But these benefits may not necessarily materialize, and Gorbachev may not be able to sustain them in the face of military logic and possible internal political and economic constraints in the Soviet Union.

c. Conventional Arms Control

In view of the most likely converging interests between the political and military leadership on nuclear arms control, what are the Soviet interests in, and what are the prospects for, conventional arms control? What, furthermore, are the chances for achieving "sensible sufficiency" in the conventional arms balance and making it impossible for the two military organizations in Europe to conduct offensive operations and launch a suprise attack?

The Soviet Union was drawn reluctantly into the talks on mutual balanced forces reductions (MBFR) in return for the Conference on Security and Cooperation in Europe (CSCE) which confirmed Soviet post-war territorial gains and frontiers. Throughout the MBFR process the Soviet Union showed no readiness to compromise on basic issues. It has insisted that there is no imbalance in forces and has refused to provide a sufficiently detailed data exchange or to agree to effective means of verification.

Under Gorbachev, the Soviet Union at the Conference on Disarmament in Europe (CDE) in Stockholm finally conceded the issue of on-site inspection. This is an important but limited step since such inspection is envisaged only in the context of notifiable activities rather that overall force levels. It is still questionable whether the Soviets would allow both the monitoring of withdrawals and thereafter regular inspection of the level of residual forces. One cannot rule out the possibility of Soviet unilateral gestures on the withdrawal of troops from Eastern Europe, as happened in 1979, but there is no guarantee that other units would not be filled out to compensate.

What is new under Gorbachev is the proposal to widen the scope of conventional arms control -- but this has been accompanied by the more traditional assertions that at present an overall balance of forces exists. Since the Budapest appeal of June 1986, Soviet military and political leaders have made repeated references to that effect.

Such statements suggest that conventional arms control discussions will be protracted and difficult, and likely to get bogged down at an early stage on the questions of data. The problem for the West is that there is no obvious military advantage to the USSR in conventional cuts -- at least not if one is thinking about reductions to common ceilings. The Soviet Union still has a need for large forces to defend its frontiers, to keep control of Eastern Europe and to fight war if necessary on two fronts. Although Moscow is certainly interested in securing nuclear reductions and constraints on SDI, it will in all likelihood refuse to sacrifice conventional superiority to this end. Concern for Soviet security and the traditionally strong influence of the ground forces in Soviet decision making on defence also place limits on the degree to which the political leadership will countenance conventional arms control as the price it has to pay for progress in other areas.

Yet another problem is that if the Soviet leadership expects that if conventional arms control proposals do come to fruition it would then be able to make the cuts from their large stocks of older equipment (e.g. T-55 tanks and MiG-21 aircraft) not later models. Only about half the Soviet tank holding is of modern versions. Such a move might cut down the Soviet inventories but it would hardly lead to major savings. On the other hand, it would mean that modernization throughout the entire range of equipment could be carried out more rapidly. And certainly the trading of vast stocks of old Soviet tanks and guns, which could be destroyed for newer NATO ones, would be an attractive proposition.

Most Soviet statements have also strongly emphasized the importance of including tactical air forces in conventional arms negotiations. Here the imbalance is less marked than in tanks. But the Soviet Union is currently reorganizing its air forces and transferring numbers of tactical aircraft to the air defence forces, which it would obviously wish to exclude from the proposals. Cuts in tactical air forces would reinforce Soviet advantages in attack helicopters and medium bombers for which there is no NATO equivalent. It would also increase the effectiveness of the Soviet air defence network which includes a large number of fixed SAM sites as well as aircraft. Of course the Soviet approach is also governed by an awareness that much of NATO's tactical nuclear delivery capability rests on dual capable aircraft, whereas for their part, the Soviets have a superiority of dual capable missile systems. They will thus probably want to retain the capability for tactical nuclear delivery.

Scepticism as to the current Soviet purposes on conventional arms control is warranted when looking at the force comparisons provided by the Soviet defence minister in February 1988.[27] The comparisons are meant to show that "violations of the military balance exist neither world wide nor in Europe". In "Europe" (including France and Spain) NATO were ahead in some categories of weapons, the Warsaw Pact in others. Thus, according to Yazov, NATO is ahead in the number

27 See *Pravda*, February 8, 1988.

of division equivalents (1.5:1), anti-tank systems (2:1), helicopters capable for combat roles (1.5:1), as well as fighter bombers and ground attack aircraft (NATO has "1 400 more attack aircraft"). The Warsaw Pact is said to be ahead only in the number of combat tanks ("20 000 more than NATO"). Equality between the two military organizations obtained in the overall number of troops in Europe and in artillery. No figures were provided for armored personnel carriers and fighter aircraft. Such force comparisons show that the data problem, so vexing at the Vienna MBFR talks, has by no means alleviated yet.

Furthermore, it is evident from Gorbachev's speech in Murmansk, in October 1987, and the submissions by General Viktor Tatarnikov, the Soviet military negotiator at the CDE talks in Stockholm, that naval forces be included in negotiations on conventional arms control. But in his listing of the balance between NATO and the Warsaw Pact, Tatarnikov alledged that NATO has a 3 to 1 advantage in naval strike vessels. Perhaps this is another area where the Soviet Union is expecting the West to make asymmetrical reductions.

Finally, whether or not a transition should be made in Soviet military doctrine, strategy and "operational art" to conventional defence with all the corresponding adjustments in the force posture, notably in Central Europe, is obviously a debatable and, in Soviet publications, contested line of development. Certainly, for a major change in doctrine to occur many internal political and military-technical obstacles would have to be overcome. And obviously, even given sufficient political power and determination to achieve such a transformation, the process of change would take a very long time.

The tendencies acting against success in conventional arms control are counteracted by Soviet economic interests. As argued above, in the short-run release of manpower can help alleviate problems caused by an acute labour shortage; transfer of resources from the military to the civilian sector can serve to reduce important bottlenecks. In the long run the channeling of scarce resources and personnel to the right sectors can aid the process of modernization and even improve economic growth. Most important of all arms control can assist in preventing an acceleration of the military-technological competition with the West.

To conclude, the Soviet motives in conventional arms control are complex. For the time being they are, among others, to engage the West in prolonged talks, with the effect of possibly reducing Western political and public support for force improvements. Ultimately, the Soviets may believe that the West will be put under pressure to make concessions and to agree to the Soviet approach of equal cuts, which would obviously at best enhance its security and at least confirm and codify the present Soviet superiority. But in the long run, failing a substantial improvement of Soviet economic performance, the Soviet Union itself may be put under more pressure to make concesssions.

On the political and military levels there are a number of specific benefits which might accrue: to cause problems within the Alliance, to reduce US force levels, and to put limits on West German forces. The extension of the scope of the talks to the Atlantic and the Urals also lets the Soviet Union off the hook over MBFR where, arguably, it has come under pressure from the West. Expansion of the forum to the CSCE format, where neutral and non-aligned states will have a say, could dilute the NATO positions.

What, finally, may be the determining factor in their approach to conventional arms control? Economically, there are definite advantages, but it would be wrong to think that at present Moscow is being forced into conventional arms control agreements by economic pressure. Militarily, there is no obvious reason to suppose that smaller forces will help Soviet security, but if cuts can be agreed on the Soviet basis, then the USSR would perhaps want to retain and possibly even enhance its present advantages. And politically, there must be considerable advantage to agreeing to talk, particularly in terms of the linkage this establishes to nuclear talks.

Hence, unless there are Soviet indications of a readiness to exchange detailed information and accept vigorous verification and, more importantly, to address some of the obvious and genuine Western security concerns over Warsaw Pact superiority, and in particular offensive capability, it is difficult to believe that conventional proposals are seriously intended as an attempt to redress existing imbalances. Therefore, whereas in the nuclear talks the military factor may be dominant in Moscow's calculations, its conventional arms control proposals at present are probably designed primarily for political purposes.

## *VI. The West and Gorbachev: Current Reactions and Future Policies*

### 1. Changes in Perception

Current Western reactions have been influenced by the developments in the Soviet Union since the fall of 1986. Initially, expectations for substantial change in Soviet policy under Gorbachev were lower than at the beginning of Andropov's rule. Disappointments could, of course, succeed the present excitement, as seems to have happened in much of Eastern Europe, e.g. in Czechoslovakia after Gorbachev's visit in April 1987. But if current trends are extrapolated, they could lead to significant shifts not only in Western views of the Soviet Union but also in Western perceptions of the security problem and of East-West relations.

On the surface, the effect of such changes should go in the direction of healing many of the rifts which have plagued the West since the decline of detente, especially concerning policy towards the Soviet Union and including such specific questions as responses to the Soviet intervention in Afghanistan after December 1979 and the "internal intervention" in Poland after December 1981, as well as the differences in attitude towards the Soviet Union between the United States and Western Europe, particularly West Germany. Today a new consensus is emerging in favour of detente and arms control, based in great part on the positive images produced by *glasnost* and by Gorbachev's peace offensive.

The only exception seems to be France. Yet one of the important effects of Gorbachev's domestic and foreign policies may be to encourage the decline of French exceptionalism. Even today, he is the first Soviet leader since Khrushchev who personally has a positive image in France. A slight majority believes in Gorbachev's genuine desire for domestic reform and for peace. For the first time in ten years, views of the Soviet Union, while still negative, have started to improve.

But there are also divisive effects of Gorbachev's policies for the West. Since Reykjavik, Western Europe has once again been under shock: after the Reagan phenomenon, the Gorbachev factor too has jolted it out of its complacency. Evidently, its groping for a positive reaction can go in two directions: that of a greater effort for West European defence cooperation and autonomy, or that of a pan-European reconciliation on the basis of denuclearization and of the overcoming of power policies. Hence a new source of division, shown by the reactions to the Washington "double zero" agreement of December 1987, could be created and exploited by Soviet policy.

Structurally, there is a certain parallelism between the new superpower detente and the intra-German rapprochement as symbolized by Honecker's visit to the Federal Republic of Germany in September 1987. What is somehow left hanging in the air is the West European dimension of East-West relations, particularly NATO's flexible response, and the French and British nuclear deterrents. To Western defence and security establishments, particularly those of France and Britain (but not necessarily to Western publics, notably the German one), the theme of ridding Europe and the world of nuclear weapons, and more generally of restructuring international relations through the power of "new thinking" and reconciliation, seems more dangerous than appealing.

Domestically, a division has been created within the conservative camp of every Western country. This has appeared spectacularly in the West German case with the divison within the government and the ruling coalition on the various "zero options". But in a more discreet way the seemingly so unshakeable French consensus has been hurt too. It may be true that the divisions have more to do with attitudes towards the American protection and pressures than with Gorbachev, but there are still considerable differences concerning the desirable response to his foreign policy initiatives between, say, West German foreign minister Genscher and French foreign minister Raimond.

On the surface everyone would probably agree with Raimond's formula of "double vigilance": to be on alert both for opportunities and for traps, and to avoid immobility as well as taking positive change for granted. The question is whether differentiation, probing and fine-tuning, which would seem to be called for, are not made doubly difficult, on the one hand, by Gorbachev's style (his dynamism and his ambiguity, his tactical flexibility and his appeal to deep-seated popular aspirations) and, on the other, the nature of the Western alliance (its diversity of interests and priorities, and its slowness in reacting and implementing concerted decisions).

Conceptually, the domestic and foreign dimensions cannot be completely separated but are not necessarily converging. Thus, for instance, Stalin and Mao Dzedung conducted moderate foreign policies at the time of these leaders' worst domestic crimes, and it was very much the latter, i.e. the negative image projected by their domestic behavior, which externally gave rise to perceptions of these leaders' "aggressive" foreign policy intentions. Conversely, Khrushchev's genuine attempts at de-Stalinization and domestic reform did not at all preclude dangerous external initiatives, e.g. in Berlin and Cuba. Finally, what is good for the Soviet people is not necessarily good for the Western alliance (see, for instance, the consequences of the death of Stalin for the European Defence Community [EDC]). Hence, it is necessary, to avoid the twin dangers of assuming that modernization or even democratization in the Soviet Union necessarily alleviates the security problem of the West and, conversely, of denying the genuine character of domestic reform in the Soviet Union for fear of encouraging illusions about Soviet power and foreign policy.

These two dangers are compounded by Gorbachev's foreign policy itself. It is based on a deft manipulation both of "openness" and "new thinking", i.e. it makes deliberate use, for Western public consumption, of (1) domestic *glasnost* and *perestroika* in order to project the image of a Soviet Union which is no longer a threat; (2) a conversion to the American themes of the post-Vietnam 1970s, including the alleged irrelevance of force in international affairs, interdependence, and the enhanced importance of regional power centres and "south-south" rather than "east-west" conflicts; (3) the West German themes of the "alternative" 1980s , such as "defensive defence", "security partnership", and "structural inability to attack"; and (4) a zest for French themes of the Gaullist 1960s, like "Europe from the Atlantic to the Ural" and "the common European house". All of these conversions probably contain a genuine element. The question is whether they are put in the service of a new foreign policy or whether, in the foreign policy area, what is new in the "new thinking" is not very credible (i.e. "a non-violent, non-nuclear world") and what is credible is not very new (i.e. "a denuclearized Europe" and a European security system replacing the two alliances).

The test, of course, does lie in the controversial question of the relation between words and deeds in Gorbachev's policies. On the genuineness of his attempt to co-operate with the United States in the Gulf, to limit involvement in the Third World, to restructure Soviet forces in Europe in a defensive direction, or to "open a new page" in the book of Soviet-West German relations, one can still legitimately argue that the change is, so far, limited to declaratory policy and contradicted by Soviet actions, or at best that the latter are beginning to change in the direction indicated by the proclamations.

What seems beyond doubt, however, is, first, that Gorbachev is ready, unlike his predecessors, to sacrifice some direct military advantages for the sake of domestic or international economic or diplomatic benefits, and, second, as Aleksandr Yakovlev put it, that the new Party leader wants to engage in an active competition with the West on the ideological and social level, i.e. those areas in which the Soviet Union previously was weak. Whether this is a substitute or only an additional means for the economic and, ultimately, the military competition remains an unanswered question which may receive different answers according to the time-frame concerned.

As shown in the preceding analytical chapters, no matter whether in the economic, the political or the military area, what Gorbachev envisages today *domestically* does represent substantial change but one that will most likely lead to a kind of "halfway house" rather than a structural revolution. At the same time they demonstrate that radical change is still possible in the future. Both developments -- the modest one for the short run, and the structural one for the long run -- do not, however, favour a maximalist interpretation: even if Gorbachev were overthrown or politically neutralized, or even if he does not go beyond the present institutional limits, the results will almost certainly not have been negative or negligible for Soviet society; conversely, a more radical reform would not necessarily spell the end of communist rule or the disintegration of the Soviet Union.

What also emerges from the above discussion of economic policies, particularly from the link between economics and defence, is that the current shifts in priority from military expenditures to industrial and technological investment could result in a stronger Soviet Union, including militarily, by the mid-1990s.

This would seem to point to important conclusions concerning the international effects of Gorbachev's policies and the desirable Western responses. There is a strong possibility of domestic and international change being correlated positively both in the short run and in the long run. In the short run, Gorbachev seems to be looking both for domestic reform and for international detente. In the long run, a successful Soviet reform which would break out of the totalitarian mould, would also mean a more stable and peaceful international environment. But on the way between present reality and distant hope, one should not minimize a serious danger: that of a Soviet leadership whose reform would be good for Soviet society, ambiguous but on balance positive for Eastern Europe, but negative for the West. That is, one needs to address the prospect of a Soviet Union made stronger, even militarily, by *perestroika* (and, perhaps, partly with the help of the West), while the West in turn would be made weaker by an exaggerated or premature perception of Soviet change, by a partial conversion to "new thinking" Gorbachev-style, and by arms control negotiations and agreements which would increase its political fragmentation and deprive it more and more of its military and technological options, including strategic defence, controlled nuclear escalation, conventional counter-offensive, land-based intermediate-range nuclear weapons, and long-range conventional missiles. The present NATO posture could be weakened while an alternative based on a second European, pillar, would be preempted.

## 2. Western European and Western Dilemmas

This is not the place to make policy recommendations; these are contained in the first part of this Report. But it is useful to point out in this concluding section some of the dilemmas which may arise when attempting to construct and implement middle or long range strategies towards the Soviet Union and Eastern Europe.

One dilemma is that of asymmetry and reciprocity. In a new era of detente and reconciliation the West must necessarily aim at reciprocity. But quite often in the past, and particularly perhaps now, the pretense of reciprocity, symmetry and commonality (as in the notion of the "common European house" and the calls for new common institutions) may serve to preserve and reinforce existing asymmetries favouring the Soviet side. But one must not obscure or overlook asymmetries, political, ideological and geographic, upon which the specific security structure of Europe is based. To that extent, aiming at real symmetry, or at least at real reciprocity, involves recognizing existing divergencies in order to overcome them.

Take, for example, arms reductions aiming at common ceilings. In this respect, Gorbachev's acceptance of the principle of asymmetric reductions is to be welcomed. But some asymmetries (like the geographic dicontinuity of the Atlantic alliance or its nuclear multipolarity) are structural and must be lived with and compensated for.

Another dilemma is that of unity and pluralism in the formulation of a coherent approach. Several eloquent papers exist which have documented the sorry state of affairs in which divergent and contradictory policies have brought the alliance. They have outlined a basic choice between pragmatism aimed at perpetuating a crumbling status quo and a long range strategy aimed at modifying the behavior of the Warsaw Pact. From such perspectives, recommendations have been derived for a comprehensive plan for arms control in Europe, but which would be part of a broader strategy aimed at inducing Soviet military self-restraint through economic incentives.

While this integrated conception should serve as a "regulatory idea" in the Kantian sense, i.e. as an inspiration for the direction in which various policies should converge, it is clear that, notwithstanding the need for Western unity and for linkage, actual policies will depend upon specific interests and contexts. Given a pluralist alliance of pluralist societies, it would not only be difficult to keep the discipline needed to maintain the conditionality necessary for global bargaining, but even more so to reach a unitary view of the objectives, the risks and the costs involved. Even on the Eastern side, whatever the centralization of the empire and the flexibility at the top, it is probably not in Gorbachev's power to deliver his side of any Grand Deal.

This is not, however, a prescription for accepting the present cacophony. Rather, the necessary -- if necessarily imperfect -- coherence should be seen as the result of a process which would start from the bottom, i.e. from the recognition, articulation and conciliation of the various perspectives, interests and priorities, national and transnational, which have emerged in recent years and have led to the well-known clashes on sanctions, on technology transfer, or on missile deployments and withdrawals.

## 3. Conclusions for Western Europe

Between the desirable comprehensive and coherent strategy for the West and the multiple ties and divisions created by cultural traditions, geopolitical location or economic interests, some bridges are needed, of which a West European point of view is probably the most natural. Precisely because Gorbachev seems to be a master in the old Soviet game of playing off Americans and Europeans, nuclear and non-nuclear proponents, Germans and French, left and right, against each other, the articulation of a conception of European perspectives and interests would be extremely useful as a guide to the actual dialogues going on between various Western and Eastern partners.

At the conceptual and global level, a West European response both to US-Soviet summit diplomacy and Gorbachev's "new thinking" would be useful. President Mitterand's speech in the *Bundestag* in 1983 and prime minister Thatcher's Moscow speech of 1987 could point the way. As expressed in these speeches, the Western Europeans should reaffirm the two essential dimensions of any international order: power and legitimacy. As against the utopia of a "non-violent" and "non-nuclear world", it should emphasize the stabilising value of the notions of balance, alliance, and deterrence, and the inevitable character of the rivalry between states and ideas. But it should welcome the emergence of a common sense of global interdependence and solidarity; and it should call for mutual tolerance and communication as a key to reconciling conflict and cooperation.

Soviet spokesmen have complained that, instead of cooperating in a restructuring of the international system, the West was calling for the restructuring of social systems, in particular the socialist ones. West Europeans should point out that, indeed, the adaptation of political regimes ot the challenges of modern society and the aspirations of peoples is the *precondition* of any meaningful transformation of the international system in a less militarized direction.

Hence, to the notion of the "common European house", West Europeans should respond by reaffirming at the same time:

- The legitimacy and value of the American alliance and physical presence.
- The right of Western Europe to its distinctive identity and defence, and its commitment to creating their political basis.
- The artificiality of Europe's division and the aspiration to undo it, through the renaissance and reinforcement of traditional human, cultural and economic ties, through collaboration in common tasks (e.g. in environmental matters) and through modern telecommunications.

These demands should not be constrained by ideological and military barriers nor swept under the rug by the euphoria of reconciliation. To reemphasize the point made earlier, neither in the case of Germany, nor in that of Central Europe and Europe as a whole, should the search for community obfuscate the ideological and political divide as well as the requirements of military balance. A full overcoming of Europe's division can only come from attacking the root both of this division and of Europe's security problem, which is neither the presence of nuclear weapons nor the superpower competition but the character of Soviet Union's military presence in, and political domination of, Eastern Europe.

# Annex: Tables

Page

*Table I** - *The Renewal of Cadres in the USSR since 1985: Gorbachev's New Appointees (May 1988)*

| Institutions | Members in May 1988 | New members compared to February 1985 | percentage of new |
|---|---|---|---|
| CC Politburo | | | |
| Members | 13 | 8 | 61.5 |
| Candidates | 7 | 5 | 71.4 |
| CC Secretaries | 13 | 10 | 76.9 |
| Heads of CC departments | 20 | 13 | 65.0 |
| Presidium of the USSR Council of Ministers[1] | 13 | 11 | 84.6 |
| Ministers of the USSR[2] | 82 | 56 | 68.2 |
| Secretaries in the Republics | 78 | 49 | 62.8 |
| among them, First Secretaries | 14 | 8 | 57.1 |
| First Secretaries of regional committees (obkom, kraikom) | 157 | 79 | 50.3 |
| Central Committee | | | |
| Members | 307 | 129 | 42.0 |
| Candidates | 161 | 110 | 68.3 |
| Auditing Committee | 84 | 63 | 75.0 |

1 This means the Chairman, First Deputy Chairmen and Deputy Chairmen of the Council of Ministers.

2 We did not include among the new ministers those who have changed porfolio between 1985 and 1988, while keeping the same status.

* These tables have been established by the SOVT computerized data bases on the Soviet Union, created by Michel Tatu and Le Monde. SOVT has memorized at this time 22,000 biographies of Soviet officials and 5,000 texts.

*Table II - Renewal Rates under Gorbachev, Brezhnev and Khrushchev (during the first three years)*

| | Gorbachev<br>Feb 85-April 88<br>% | Brezhnev<br>Sep 64-Nov 67<br>% | Khrushchev<br>March 53-April 56<br>% |
|---|---|---|---|
| **Politburo**[1] | | | |
| Members | 61.5 | 36.3 | 25.0 |
| Candidates | 83.3 | 100.0 | 83.3 |
| **Secretaries** | 76.9 | 55.5 | 62.5 |
| **Central Committee** | | | |
| Members | 42.0 | 27.8 | 40.1 |
| Candidates | 68.3 | 56.7 | 61.4 |

1 The Politburo (named Presidium in the fifties and up to 1966) had been considerably enlarged at the XIXth Congress, in October 1952. As soon as Stalin died in March 1953, his heirs had put an end to this anomaly by restoring the "hard core" of the Politburo of the fourties. We have considered only this "small composition" as far as March 1953 is concerned.

*Table III - The Central Committee Elected in March 1986*

| | March 1986 (27th Congress) | % | March 1981 (26th Congress) | % |
|---|---|---|---|---|
| **Full members**, total[1] | 307 | 100.0 | 319 | 100.0 |
| among them: | | | | |
| - entirely news | 94 | 30.6 | 41 | 12.8 |
| - previously candidates | 23 | 7.5 | 36 | 11.2 |
| - previously members of the Auditing Committee | 8 | | 5 | |
| - old members | 182 | 59.2 | 238 | 74.3 |
| **How many were already full members:** | | | | |
| - 5 years earlier | 172 | 56.0 | 232 | 72.5 |
| - 10 years earlier | 112 | 36.4 | 154 | 48.1 |
| - 15 years earlier | 61 | 19.8 | 86 | 26.8 |
| - 20 years earlier | 29 | 9.4 | 55 | 17.2 |
| - 25 years earlier | 19 | 6.2 | 17 | 5.3 |
| - 30 years earlier | 6 | 1.9 | 12 | 3.7 |
| **Age:** | | | | |
| - more than 70 | 33 | 10.7 | 54 | 16.8 |
| - 60 to 70 | 94 | 30.6 | 117 | 36.5 |
| - 50 to 60 | 145 | 47.2 | 120 | 37.5 |
| - less than 50 | 33 | 10.7 | 24 | 7.5 |
| **Women:** | 13 | 4.2 | 8 | 2.5 |
| **Functions:** | | | | |
| - In the party: | | | | |
| . central apparatus | 28 | 9.1 | 27 | 8.4 |
| . in the apparatus of the Republics | 20 | 6.5 | 21 | 6.5 |
| . regional secretaries | 78 | 25.4 | 82 | 25.7 |
| - In the Government: | | | | |
| . Council of Ministers of USSR | 75 | 24.4 | 81 | 25.3 |
| . Diplomacy | 14 | 4.5 | 16 | 5.0 |
| . Military | 23 | 7.5 | 23 | 7.2 |
| . KGB and MVD | 6 | 1.9 | 6 | 1.9 |
| **Members of the USSR Academy of Sciences** | 17 | 5.5 | 19 | 5.9 |
| **Holders of University titles**[2] | 54 | 17.5 | 65 | 20.3 |
| **Where they have functions:** | | | | |
| - in Central Asia | 13 | 4.2 | 18 | 5.6 |
| - Transcaucasia | 3 | | 4 | |
| - Baltic States | 3 | | 4 | |

1 The total number here is the one registered right after the election in March 1986; it is different from the total put in other tables for the date of May 1988, due to deceases, exclusions and promotions from candidates decided after the Congress.

2 Professor, "kandidat", doctor, "dotsent" or "aspirant".

*Table IV - The Renewal of Central Committee Since Lenin's Death*

| Date of the Congresses | Number of full members in the CC | New | %[1] | Old | %[2] |
|---|---|---|---|---|---|
| May 1924 (13th Congress) | 53 | 17 | 32.0 | 36 | 90.0 |
| December 1925 (14th) | 63 | 18 | 28.5 | 45 | 84.9 |
| December 1927 (15th) | 71 | 21 | 29.5 | 50 | 79.3 |
| July 1930 (16th) | 71 | 17 | 23.9 | 54 | 76.0 |
| February 1934 (17th) | 71 | 21 | 29.5 | 50 | 70.4 |
| March 1939 (18th) | 71 | 55 | 77.4 | 16 | 22.5 |
| October 1952 (19th)[3] | 126 | 90 | 71.4 | 26 | 50.7 |
| February 1956 (20th) | 132 | 53 | 40.0 | 79 | 62.6 |
| October 1961 (22th)[4] | 175 | 110 | 62.8 | 65 | 49.2 |
| April 1966 (23rd) | 195 | 55 | 28.2 | 140 | 80.0 |
| April 1971 (24th) | 240 | 92 | 38.3 | 148 | 75.8 |
| March 1976 (25th) | 287 | 86 | 29.9 | 201 | 83.7 |
| April 1981 (26th) | 319 | 89 | 27.8 | 230 | 80.1 |
| March 1986 (27th) | 307 | 125 | 40.7 | 182 | 57.0 |

1 We considered as new the full members who had not this position before, even when they were candidate members or members of the Auditing Committee. The percentage of new members is calculated by comparison to the total number of full members of the *given* year.

2 The "old" members are those who were reelected into the same position. Their percentage is calculated in relation with the total of full members at the *last* election.

3 We did not take into accounte the 28th Party conference, hold in February 1941, who changed slightly the composition of the CC, notably by adding four new members.

4 The 21st Congress was hold in January-February 1959, but it was "extraordinary" and did not hold an election.

*Table V - The "Stagnation Rate"*

| Functions | total in May 1988 | held the same position: in February 1985 | | in October 1982 | |
|---|---|---|---|---|---|
| | | 1985 | % | 1982 | % |
| Politburo: | | | | | |
| - Members | 13 | 5 | 38.4 | 3 | 23.0 |
| - Candidates | 7 | 2 | 28.5 | 2 | 28.5 |
| Secretariat | 13 | 3 | 23.0 | 2 | 15.3 |
| Heads of CC departments | 20 | 7 | 35.0 | 2 | 10.0 |
| Presidum of the USSR Council of Ministers | 13 | 2 | 15.3 | 1 | 7.6 |
| Ministers of the USSR | 82 | 26 | 31.7 | 16 | 19.5 |
| Secretaries of the Republics | 78 | 29 | 37.1 | 20 | 25.6 |
| among them: | | | | | |
| First Secretaries | 14 | 6 | 42.8 | 4 | 28.5 |
| Regional First Secretaries (obkoms and kraikoms) | 157 | 78 | 49.6 | 47 | 29.9 |
| Central Committee | | | | | |
| Members | 307 | 178 | 57.9 | 171 | 55.7 |

*Table VI - Regional Inertia*
*The Renewal Rate in the Republics (in decreasing order)*

| | How many people are new (in May 1988) Compared to February 1985 (percentage) | | |
|---|---|---|---|
| | Republican Secretaries | Member of local CC | obkom first secretaries |
| Kazakhstan | 100.0 | 71.2 | 52.6 |
| Uzbekistan | 100.0 | 77.9 | 53.8 |
| Tadzhikistan | 100.0 | 61.5 | 75.0 |
| Kirquizia | 80.0 | 62.5 | 75.0 |
| Turkmenistan | 80.0 | 63.6 | 80.0 |
| Armenia* | 66.6 | 48.4 | ---- |
| Latvia* | 60.0 | 54.4 | ---- |
| Lituania | 60.0 | 42.4 | ---- |
| Estonia* | 60.0 | 42.5 | ---- |
| Moldavia* | 60.0 | 45.6 | ---- |
| Georgia | 50.0 | 50.3 | 33.3 |
| Bielorussia | 50.0 | 62.2 | 50.0 |
| Ukraine* | 28.5 | 44.6 | 36.0 |
| Azerbaidzhan* | 16.6 | 48.9 | ---- |
| RSFSR | ---- | ---- | 50.0 |

* This sign indicates that the First Secretary of the Republic is the same as in February 1985.

Several Republics are not divided into regions. The Russian Republic (RSFSR) has the biggest number of regions, but it has no Central Committee nor a special secretariat.

*Table VII - The New Appointees and Their Age*

| | GORBACHEV'S EARLY PERIOD (Feb 1985 - May 1987) | | | | | BREZHNEV'S EARLY PERIOD (Sept 1964 - Oct 1967) | | | | |
|---|---|---|---|---|---|---|---|---|---|---|
| | Total[1] | age in 1988 | | | | Total[1] | age in 1967 | | | |
| | | <50 | 50-60 | 60-70 | >70 | | <50 | 50-60 | 60-70 | >70 |
| The new members of: | | | | | | | | | | |
| the Politburo: | | | | | | | | | | |
| - full members | 8/13 | - | 4 | 4 | - | 4/11 | 1 | 2 | 1 | - |
| - candidates | 5/7 | - | 3 | 2 | - | 6/9 | 3 | 3 | - | - |
| the Secretariat | 10/13 | - | 7 | 3 | - | 5/9 | 1 | 3 | 1 | - |
| the Presidium of the USSR Council of Ministers | 11/13 | | 8 | 3 | - | 5/12 | 1 | 4 | - | - |
| TOTAL | 34/46 | | 22 | 12 | - | 20/41 | 6 | 12 | 2 | |
| Percentage[2] | 73.9 | | 64.7 | 35.2 | | 48.7 | 30 | 60 | 10 | |
| The CC (full members) | 129/307 | 18 | 73 | 32 | 3 | 54/191 | 12 | 32 | 9 | - |
| Percentage[2] | 42 | 14 | 56.5 | 24.8 | | 28.2 | 22 | 59 | 16 | |

1 The first figure indicates how many members are new compared to the total (second figure, preceded by /) of the given institution in July 1987 and in January 1967 respectively.

2 The figure in the Column "total" gives the proportion of new members in the given institutions. Figures in other columns give the proportion of each age category among these new members.

Rolf Ahmann

# Nichtangriffspakte: Entwicklung und operative Nutzung in Europa 1922-1939

## Mit einem Ausblick auf die Renaissance des Nichtangriffsvertrages nach dem Zweiten Weltkrieg

---

»Die Regierungen schreiben Nichtangriffspakte. Kleiner Mann schreibe dein Testament« (Berthold Brecht). Fast gleichzeitig mit der Entstehung des Begriffes »Sicherheitspolitik« wurde nach dem Ersten Weltkrieg ein neues vertragspolitisches Instrument entwickelt, das in Europa bis 1939 eine umfassende Verbreitung und nach 1945 weltweit eine Renaissance erlebte: der »reine« Nichtangriffsvertrag. Da zumeist trotz vorhandener Friedensverträge und ohne kriegerische Konflikte vorgeschlagen und abgeschlossen, begleitete diese Verträge schon früh die Frage nach ihrem Sinn und Nutzen, provozierten sie extrem gegengesetzte Bewertungen.

Wann, wo und wie entstanden Nichtangriffsverträge? Was waren ihre Inhalte und Unterschiede? Wer verwendete, unter welchen Rahmenbedingungen, mit welchen Zielen und Konzeptionen diese Verträge? Was und wie war ihre operative Nutzung im politischen, wirtschaftlichen und militärstrategischen Bereich?

Die interdisziplinäre Studie, die zugleich eine Geschichte des Angriffsverzichts in der Neuzeit bietet, konzentriert sich auf die beiden ersten und umfangreichsten Systeme derartiger Verträge bis 1939, das sowjetische und das deutsche. Außer der sowjetischen und der deutschen bezieht die Arbeit die Außenpolitik zahlreicher anderer Staaten in Europa und Asien in die Analyse ein. Die Studie verdeutlicht Grundelemente der »Nichtangriffspaktpolitik« bis in die unmittelbare Gegenwart.

*1988, 764 S., Salesta geb., 89,- DM,* ISBN 3-7890-1387-0
(Internationale Politik und Sicherheit, Band 23)

Hannes Adomeit

# Die Sowjetmacht in internationalen Krisen und Konflikten

## Verhaltensmuster, Handlungsprinzipien, Bestimmungsfaktoren mit einem Vorwort von Richard Löwenthal

Ein besseres Verständnis der Gründe und Verhaltensmuster sowjetischen Vorgehens erfordert eine theoretische Klärung eines analytischen Konzepts außenpolitischen Handelns mit dem Gesichtspunkt der Risikobereitschaft im Mittelpunkt sowie die Sichtung gängiger Thesen zum Krisen- und Konfliktverhalten der Sowjetunion.
Behandelt werden u. a.: Die Blockade Berlins, der Bau der Mauer und die Stationierung von Raketen auf Kuba als auch das Eingreifen in Ungarn, die Intervention in der ČSSR und die Besetzung Afghanistans. Auch die plötzliche Entschärfung schwebender Krisen wie der Truppenabzug aus dem Iran 1946, der Verzicht auf militärische Gegenmaßnahmen bei der amerikanischen Blockade der nordvietnamesischen Häfen im Mai 1972 oder das Ausbleiben einer militärischen Intervention in Polen 1980–81.
Mögliche verhaltensbestimmende Faktoren (Ideologie, nationale Interessen, militärische Macht, innenpolitische Verhältnisse) werden herausgearbeitet und sich im Krisenverlauf verändernde Handlungsweisen ausgewertet. Im letzten Teil des Buches wird das sowjetische Vorgehen in Ost-Mitteleuropa unter Stalin und Chruščev miteinander verglichen und zum Verhalten der UdSSR in anderen geographischen Räumen sowie unter Breznev in Bezug gesetzt.

*1983, 496 S., 15,3 x 22,7 cm, Salesta geb., 49,– DM* ISBN 3–7890–0812–5
(Internationale Politik und Sicherheit, Band 20)

**NOMOS VERLAGSGESELLSCHAFT**
**Postfach 610 · 7570 Baden-Baden**